On the Trail of Whales

To Jonas Spinoy, Jennifer Amengual, and Quentin Oliveira,
hoping they will have seen many more whales.

Graphic design and layout: Pierre Dusser
Maps: Noël Blotti
Americanization: Nicole Valaire

Series produced by Cap Nature

First edition for the United States
published by Barron's Educational Series, Inc., 1998

First published in 1997 in France by Editions Nathan, Paris, France.

All inquiries should be addressed to:
Barron's Educational Series, Inc.
250 Wireless Boulevard
Hauppauge, New York 11788
http://www.barronseduc.com

International Standard Book No. 0-7641-0598-1

Library of Congress Catalog Card No. 98-4550

Library of Congress Cataloging-in-Publication Data
Dumont, Jean-Michel, 1955–
 [Cap sur les baleines. English]
 On the trail : whales/Jean-Michel Dumont, Rémy Marion;
illustrations by François Desbordes. — 1st ed. for the U.S.
  p.   cm.
 Includes index.
 ISBN 0-7641-0598-1
  1. Whales.   I. Marion, Rémy.   II. Title.
 QL737.C4D834 1998
 599.5—dc21
                                                       98-4550
                                                          CIP

PRINTED IN ITALY

987654321

On the Trail of Whales

Jean-Michel Dumont and Rémy Marion

Illustrations by François Desbordes

BARRON'S
Nature Travel Guides

Contents

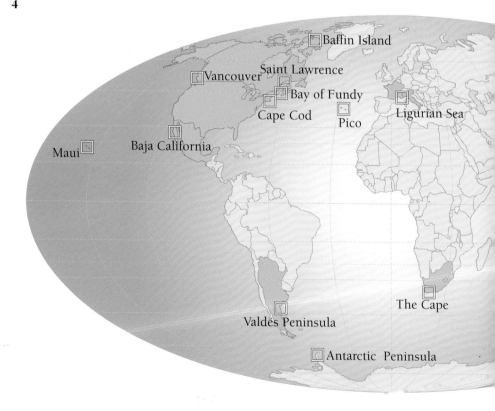

5

Nullarbor
Kaikoura

WITHDRAWN

Foreword

Going out to sea to watch whales is an unforgettable experience. Getting close to some of the largest animals that have ever existed on earth is an absolutely unique opportunity.

The sites described in this field guide will give you a chance to see the species during the months we suggest. If you don't see any whales on an outing, most whale-watching organizations will take you out on a second trip. This book also highlights the fauna, flora, geology, and history of each whale-watching region.

This guide is not exhaustive. We do not discuss places where systematic whale-watching is not certain. We also do not discuss whale species that are only rarely seen.

For many centuries, people hunted whales. Today, people are becoming increasingly interested in learning about whales. The aim of this book is to help people find and come close to whales.

On the trail of whales!

Origin, evolution, and classification

Whales belong to a group of mammals called cetaceans, which are large sea animals. Whales are mammals that used to live on land. They began to live in the sea tens of millions of years ago. *Pakicetus* is their oldest known ancestor. It was found in Pakistan, which was under the sea at the beginning of the Eocene period, 55 million years ago. Only its head was found, so we don't know if this was a marine animal that had not yet developed all of the characteristics of whales—such as hearing under water, or echolocation—or one of the whale's last amphibious ancestors.

Lots of true whale fossils have been found in the mid-Eocene period—45 million years ago—in Egypt, Nigeria, Louisiana, Alabama, and South Carolina. These whales are called archaeocetes, and could be up to 69 feet long (21 m). Included in the archaeocetes were the basilosaurs, which had a much longer body than today's whales, as well as the dorudons, protocetes, and patriocetes, which probably looked very much like today's whales. *Basilosaurus's* head was still relatively small, representing only 7.5 percent of its total length, but *Protocetus's* head was up to 24 percent of its length, which is comparable to contemporary whales. In *Pakicetus*, the blowhole still resembled nostrils; however, in

10

archaeocetes, the blowhole was halfway between the front and the back of its head. Archaeocetes' teeth were like those of primitive mammals, with 44 teeth differentiated into incisors and canines—which were uniradicular—as well as premolars and molars—which were pluri-radicular. The presence of these different teeth means that they were "heterodontal" whales. Their front legs had already developed into flippers whereas, at least in some species, the back legs still existed, though much smaller, and were still jointed with a pelvis that was no longer attached to

Basilosaur bones and other fossils dating from the Eocene period, about 40 million years ago, have been found in the western Egyptian desert.

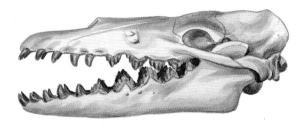

Basilosaur teeth were still clearly differentiated, whereas the nostrils had begun to move toward the top of the skull.

A complete basilosaur skeleton. Scientists recently established that basilosaurs actually had back legs that had been greatly reduced in size but were still functional. They may have been used to facilitate copulation (drawing adapted from Gingerich et al.).

Ichthyosaurs and whales: evolutionary similarities and differences

Ichthyosaurs were reptiles that had become completely aquatic. Like whales, they probably developed from animals that had once lived on land. Even though ichthyosaurs and whales do not share a common ancestor, they have a number of similar evolutionary developments, such as the loss of mobility of the vertebrae in the neck and the separation of the pelvis from the spinal column.

Ichthyosaurs, like whales, have a hyperphalanging of the flippers and, though less pronounced than in whales, their blowholes have moved towards the back. Though their general appearance is fairly similar, there are, of course, significant differences between them, particularly in regard to their flippers. An ichthyosaur's tail fluke moved from side to side, like a fish's tail. An ichthyosaur's spinal column ended in the lower tail fluke, making it stiff. A whale tail fluke moves up and down and has no bone structure. The back legs in ichthyosaurs developed into fins. In whales, the back legs no longer exist. Some whales have internal remnants of their back legs that are used as anchoring points for male reproductive organs.

Ichthyosaurs and whales have one other characteristic in common—they both lived in the same ecological niche. Whales now live in the ecological niche that became available when the ichthyosaurs disappeared.

Drawing caption: Unlike modern-day whales, the ichthyosaur had back legs that had clearly developed into flippers (Drawing adapted from Stromer).

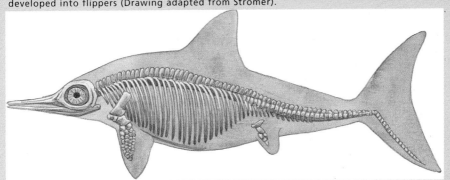

11

the spinal column.

The archaeocetes reached their peak during the Oligocene period, about 30 million years ago. They completely disappeared about 20 million years ago, at the beginning of the Miocene period. The Oligocene period was the Golden Age of whales, in which many species coexisted. Today, whales are divided into two main groups: odontocetes, which are whales that have teeth, and are called toothed whales; and mysticetes, which are whales with baleen plates instead of teeth, and are called baleen whales.

Toothed whales

The first toothed whales were differentiated from the archaeocetes by the development on the front of their skulls of an organ mainly used in the process of navigating by sound, called the melon. This is a mass of oil forming a lens that focuses the audible "clicks" that whales emit. Whales send out

these sounds that bounce off objects around them. These echoes can tell whales a lot about their surroundings. This is called echolocation. Some toothed whales have an extremely acute sense of hearing using echolocation.

Appearing at the end of the Eocene, the first toothed whales were called squalodonts. These were the last of the heterodontal toothed whales. Their teeth were still very much like those of most land mammals, and probably allowed them to catch, filter, grind, and tear their food to pieces, all at the same time. Their diet was probably a fairly varied one.

Their teeth gradually developed from heterodontal to homodontal. All modern-day whales have teeth that are simplified, uniradical, and virtually all alike. They are used only to catch prey, which is swallowed whole. The number of teeth varies considerably according to the species and the individual, ranging from a single tooth in the male narwhal—a homodontal whale that is particularly oligodontal (having few teeth)— to 260 in some dolphins, which are all polyodontal. Today, the suborder of toothed whales is subdivided into 66 species grouped into five families. One of these families, the physeters, has existed since the early Miocene, and includes the largest species of toothed whales, the sperm whale.

Baleen Whales

Baleen whales first appeared during the Oligocene. They have extremely large jaws, and are distinguishable from other whales because their teeth have been replaced with baleen plates.

As embryos, baleen whales develop lots of identical tooth buds, which are reabsorbed prior to birth. Baleen plates then appear during the first six months after birth. Baleen plates are made out of keratin and form a fringe that traps tiny organisms.

Baleen plates hang from a whale's jaw. They are generally spaced at least 1/2 inch apart (less than 1 cm). The number of baleen goes from 320 in the gray whale to 720 in the fin whale. Bowhead whale baleen plates are the longest at 14.8 feet (4.5 m). Baleen plates are often referred to as whalebone due

12

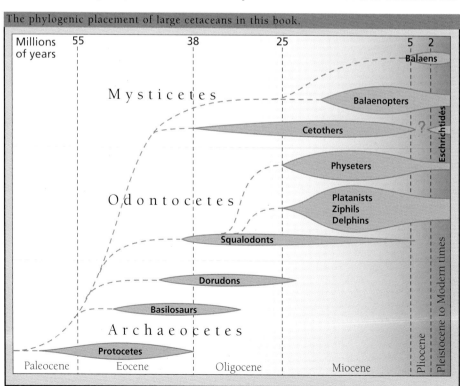

The phylogenic placement of large cetaceans in this book.

| Millions of years | 55 | 38 | 25 | 5 | 2 |

Paleocene | Eocene | Oligocene | Miocene | Pliocene | Pleistocene to Modern times

to their horny and stiff texture. In some whales, baleen is white, while in others it can be black, yellow, or even two-toned. The plates are arranged side by side with a smooth edge facing toward the outside of the mouth and a fibrous edge facing in. The fibrous edge has hairlike bristles that point down along the baleen's length. The prey gets caught on the hairlike bristles and then the whale uses its tongue to clean the food off of its baleen and to its throat. Since baleen plates wear with use, they continue to grow throughout the whale's life. Baleen whales are able to filter water using their baleen plates, which means they can eat all sorts of small prey. Their basic diet consists of plankton, shellfish, small squid, sprats, anchovies, capelins, herring, and mackerel. They sometimes also eat gulls or penguins that have come to fish in the middle of the whale's meal.

The modern-day suborder of baleen whales is divided into three families.

The oldest family is probably the eschrichtius, which are very similar to the cetothers that appeared at the beginning of the Oligocene. Today, this family includes only one species—the gray whale. The gray whale has traits that are halfway between the two other, more recent families. Its body is less streamlined than that of the rorquals but less thickset than that of the right whales. Its rostrum is not as straight as a rorqual's rostrum, but is not as curved as a right whale's. It has the beginnings of a dorsal fin and two folds under the throat, instead of the ventral grooves that are on rorquals. Its baleen plates are short, and it has fewer baleen plates than other baleen whales. A second family, the balaens, have a thickset shape. A balaen's head can represent up to 40 percent of its total length. It has a highly arched rostrum, long baleen plates, and no dorsal fin. The balaen family is made up of two species—the right whale and the bowhead whale.

The third family, the balaenopters, encompasses the most species. A balaenopter has a very hydrodynamic body, a straight rostrum, short baleen plates, and dozens of distinct ventral grooves. The balaenopter family includes rorquals, which all have long, streamlined bodies and short flippers, as well as megapters, or humpback whales, which have less streamlined bodies and long flippers.

Description

Nervous system, brain, and senses

Scientists have known for a long time that the weight of the brain is not in and of itself a measure of intelligence; however, the relationship between the brain and body weight is relevant. This relationship varies according to the whale species but it is clearly different between the two suborders. Baleen whales have a relatively small brain. It represents only 1/20,000th of a blue whale's body. A toothed whale's brain is proportionally much bigger, ranging from 1/4,000th in the sperm whale to 1/76th in the tersiops dolphin, considered to be one of the most intelligent animals. A human brain is about 1/50th of a person's weight.

Studies of different parts of the brain show the relative importance of the five senses in whales. A marked feature of all whale brains is the importance of the areas for hearing. On the other hand, the areas for smelling, still present in the archaeocetes, are considerably reduced in the baleen whales and have completely disappeared in toothed whales. Vision, which is rather good in all whales, is monocular. A whale's eyes are small, and are located on either side of the animal. Each eye's field of vision does not overlap with the other eye. Whales seem to have a sense of touch throughout their bodies as well as in hairs located around the mouth. The sense of taste seems to have disappeared.

Skeleton

Whale skeletons are very different from the skeletons of other mammals. A whale's skeleton does not have to support the animal's weight. The skeleton only has to provide points of attachment for the muscles. The difference from other mammals is particularly evident in the skull. The nasal bones have moved to the top of the head, which makes it easier for whales to breathe at the water's surface. The maxillary and premaxillary bones are considerably longer. This change in shape of a whale's skull does not happen until late in the development of the embryo. It is caused by the uneven growth of the various bones in the head. All toothed whales show a more or less marked asymmetry of the skull depending on the species and the individual. This asymmetry is especially obvious in the nasal passages,

13

which systematically move toward the left. Whale bones are fairly light. With the exception of certain extremely dense bones in the skull, whale bones consist of a thin, compact envelope surrounding a delicate spongy structure filled with particularly fatty marrow which represents approximately 50 percent of the bone. The fat contained in the bones reduces the overall density enough that the bones can often float. The skeleton represents about 17 percent of a whale's total weight.

The spinal column is also very different from that of other mammals. Depending on the species, some or all of the cervical vertebrae are welded to each other, which limits the mobility of the skull. The seven cervical vertebrae that all mammals have are unattached in the fin whale, but most others have some or all fused, such as the right whale and dwarf sperm.

Most whales have between 12 to 13 pairs of ribs that do not connect to the sternum, but some have more. The pygmy right whale has 17 pairs of broadly shaped ribs. In baleen whales, usually the first pair of ribs connects with the one small bone that is the sternum. In toothed whales, however, the sternum is made of a few bones and more ribs connect to it with bony segments called sternal ribs.

Fin whale skeleton.

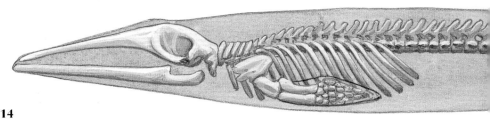

Right whale skeleton.

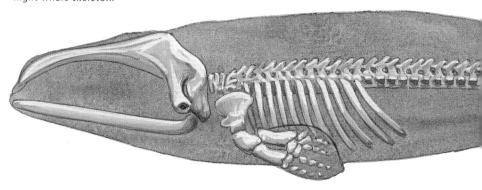

Sperm whale skeleton.

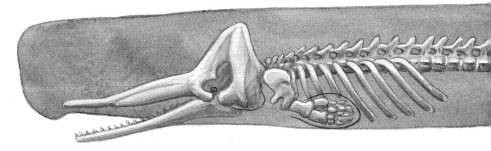

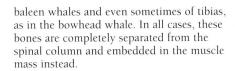

The two flippers have a structure that is close to that of land mammals. They are jointed with the shoulder blades, but there is no clavicle. As opposed to most other mammals, the arm is shorter and the hand longer. The four or five fingers on the hand have developed into a flipper that includes many phalanges—up to eight in the third digit of the humpback whale.

A whale skeleton is also different from those of other mammals because of the disappearance, or nearly complete disappearance, of the pelvis. Due to evolution, it sometimes exists in a vestigial state, accompanied by rudimentary femurs in baleen whales and even sometimes of tibias, as in the bowhead whale. In all cases, these bones are completely separated from the spinal column and embedded in the muscle mass instead.

Organs that do not exist in any other mammal

All whales have tails that are divided by a notch into two lobes, each called a fluke. Therefore, a whale's tail has two flukes. It moves up and down, instead of side to side like those of fish, and is used to propel a whale forward. It does not have any bones in it and has nothing to do with the absent rear limbs. Most large whales use their flukes to swim at a leisurely four to five miles per hour, but some can swim at about twenty miles per hour for a short time. The flukes of some species, such as the humpback, have coloration or scarring patterns that are unique to each individual. These characteristics have allowed scientists to identify and monitor the behavior of many individual whales.

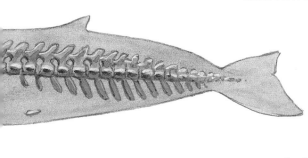

Except for right whales, narwhals, and belugas, which live in seas filled with sheets of ice, as well as some dolphins, whales are also the only mammals to have a dorsal fin. The dorsal fin also does not have any bones in it, and is used to maintain stability while swimming.

The keen hearing of whales

Air has a very different density from that of a mammal's body. Sounds usually reach the auditory nerve only through the ears, which allow for stereoscopic hearing. Water, however, has a density close to that of the body. A mammal normally cannot pinpoint the origin of sounds because they are spread directly through it, reaching the auditory nerves simultaneously from all directions. Whales have overcome this problem by developing both a pneumatic cavity isolating the auditory region from the rest of the skull and a tympanic bubble with a very high density that acts inside tissue as would an ear trumpet in the open air. Since the internal ears are separated from each other by their peribular sinuses, and the tympanic bubbles receive sound waves independently

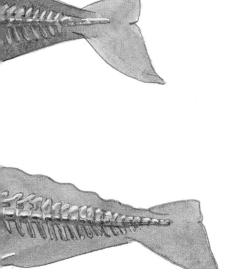

15

from each side of the skull, hearing, although under water, once again becomes directional.

The density of the other bones in the tympanum is another barrier to the transmission of sound to the internal ear, since sound waves have great difficulty communicating between areas with different density. Finally, to deal with the enormous variations of pressure during diving, the sinus also contains a cavity that fills with blood in order to equalize pressure.

The fact that this evolution of the auditory apparatus, which occurs in both the baleen whales and the toothed whales, does not occur in any other mammal, even aquatic, is a decisive argument in favor of the unique origin of all whales. The study of the auditory apparatus of whales shows, however, that the auditory apparatus of baleen whales is less developed than that of toothed whales. This has been confirmed by calculations based on the range of sounds they produce and their respective auditory range. The auditory range of most baleen whales goes up to at least 12.5 to 32,000 Hz, while that of some toothed whales probably reaches 200,000 Hz. For humans, the range is 30 to 16,000 Hz. Even without external ears, all whales have keen hearing. It is by far the most important of their senses. The sounds produced by whales seem to have two purposes—communicating and perceiving their surroundings using echolocation. Sounds of less than 1,000 Hz are probably communication vectors—the more muted they are, the further they can go. For example, a sound signal of 20 Hz with a wavelength of about 245 feet (75 m) will only be stopped by obstacles with a larger diameter. Male humpback whales will sometimes emit low frequency sounds for up to 20 hours, only taking short breaks for breathing. This

16

"song" is believed to be used to entice a mate and its characteristics can change from year to year. Muted sounds are of little use for echolocation; however, if they are emitted forcefully, they can travel quickly—up to five times the speed of sound in air—over distances of several hundred miles. All large whales, from baleen whales to sperm whales, produce sounds in the 12.5 to 1,000 band.

Echolocation requires sharper sounds. We are now well aware of the astonishing sound range of small-toothed whales. Some of them are able to produce sounds reaching 200,000 Hz. With the exception of right whales, which seem to be silent beyond 2,000 Hz, other baleen whales and the sperm whale produce sounds up to 32,000 Hz. We are now fairly certain that sperm whales, which, like other toothed whales, have a melon and feed on large prey at depths beyond the reach of light, also use echolocation. The melon, which is made of oily and fibrous tissue, apparently helps dolphins and other

Gray whale seen from the front. It has a huge tongue, and its baleen plates are short.

toothed whales to focus the sounds that they emit for echolocation. The use of echolocation in rorquals has not been proven, but it is possible that these baleen whales use it to locate schools of fish that they feed on when they dive.

Adapting to marine life

Of all marine mammals, whales are the most advanced in their adaptation to living in water. Externally, their bodies are well-adapted to the constraints of their environment. To overcome water resistance, a whale has a hydrodynamic body in which all of the bumps have been erased. Body hair has practically disappeared while teats and genital organs are situated in longitudinal grooves to avoid eddies. The skin itself is completely bare and covered with an oily film. It has the consistency of a hard-boiled egg out of its shell. The skin and underlying blubber is firm but pliable. It has been observed that as whales change speed or direction small folds occur in the skin. The folds may help to reduce drag by decreasing the amount of turbulence that is created along the skin. Whales live in an environment that has a temperature that is less than their own internal temperature and that conducts heat 27 times better than air. Whales have developed ways to protect themselves against heat loss. They have a thick layer of blubber, which, coupled with the shape of a whale, offers practically the smallest possible area for

heat exchange. Sweat glands play an essential role in regulation for land mammals. Whales don't have sweat glands. Whales maintain a constant internal temperature using their heavily veined flippers and tail fluke. Blood vessels can contract or dilate as needed. Heat is conserved through countercurrent heat exchange as well. In this adaptation, blood traveling in the arteries toward the extremities loses some of its heat to the blood returning in the adjacent veins. Many kinds of mammals have this heat conservation strategy, but in whales it is modified. The arteries going to the extremities and the returning veins are kept together by tissue in a plexus, or bundle, where heat is exchanged more efficiently.

The requirements for diving have caused adaptations in how whales store oxygen. Whale lungs are extremely efficient and permit gas exchanges much more quickly than the lungs of any other mammal. The lungs of whales are not relatively larger than those of land mammals, but they exchange more air with each breath. Whales exchange about 80 percent of their lung capacity compared to about 30 percent for land mammals. This allows large whales to spend a half hour or an hour under water after only a few minutes on the surface. Their blood stores proportionally more oxygen than ours does. Whales have double the number of red corpuscles per unit of blood that we do and they also have, proportional to their size, a third more blood. However, it is mainly their muscles, which have a very high concentration of myoglobin, that absorb the oxygen they need to be active under water. Myoglobin, massively present in whale muscles, plays the same role as hemoglobin in the blood and gives a whale's meat its almost black color. In addition to their ability to store oxygen, whales are able to drastically limit oxygen consumption while under water. The vasoconstriction of most of the circulatory system and the slowing down of the pulse reduces the circulation of blood, which tends to be limited to the irrigation of vital organs, such as the brain

17

Characteristic blow of a humpback whale off the coast of New England.

and heart, while the muscles function by only using oxygen contained in their myoglobin. The fact that air consists not only of oxygen but also of nitrogen causes problems under water. Whales have developed original solutions that are not completely clear. We know that whales maintain very little air in their respiratory system when they are under water. Their fairly supple skeletons allow their lungs to completely collapse under pressure. The other passages and sinuses of their lungs are covered with a mucus that is rich in fat, which absorbs the nitrogen, rendering it harmless as the whale quickly resurfaces. It is the presence of this mucus in the whale's blow that partially explains why a whale's blow is always visible, regardless of the external temperature. The other reason is that this humid blow reacts exactly like any gas that suddenly dilates while cooling off, causing the water it contains to condense.

Paradoxically, the return to an exclusively marine life created another problem for whales—the risk of death by dehydration. Fortunately, since they no longer have sweat glands, whales need a lot less water than land mammals of the same size. They also have kidneys that are comparatively much larger and more sophisticated, which enable them to eliminate extra salt in extremely concentrated urine.

Way of life

Food

Sperm whales are the largest of the toothed whales. Their diet is primarily teuthophagic, which means it consists primarily of squid. The whale swallows all squid whole.

Baleen whales, on the other hand, feed by filtering large quantities of water through their baleen plates, which retain their prey. Each baleen whale family has its own specific feeding behavior.

Gray whales, the only members of the eschrichtius family, feed primarily by raking sediment on the ocean floor to extract mollusks and shellfish.

Right whales, members of the balaen family, mainly feed by moving through water with their mouths open. The water enters the mouth from the front through a gap in the baleen plates and is then forced by the

18

Group of fin whales feeding on a school of herring.

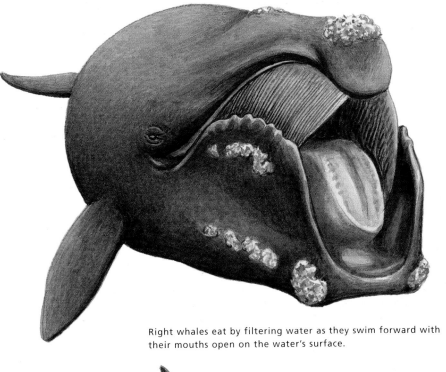

Right whales eat by filtering water as they swim forward with their mouths open on the water's surface.

Rorquals (here, a minke whale) open their mouths and let the water filter through them.

whale's motion out the side of the mouth through the long baleen plates, up to 12 feet long.

The various rorqual whales and humpback whales that make up the balaenopter family swim forward with open mouths into schools of krill or fish. The throats of these whales can be enlarged because the throat has longitudinal grooves that can expand. The whale releases the muscles in its throat, which becomes a huge sac. By closing its mouth and contracting its muscles, a balaenopter filters the contents of its throat so as to ingest only food that has been trapped in its baleen plates. Some baleen whale species have been observed hunting cooperatively to concentrate prey into a small area. Fin and humpback whales may use their bodies to corral fish into a tight school and humpback whales have even been observed using bubbles to achieve this. They dive under a school of fish and release a stream of small bubbles that scares the fish into a tighter group. Once the fish are concentrated together the whales lunge in with mouths open.

Surprisingly, a whale's stomach consists of several chambers. This has led several scientists to propose the theory of a common ancestor for whales and ruminants (a thesis that reinforces some studies on DNA in these two orders). The first chamber is a muscular extension of the esophagus in which the food is ground. In the second chamber, gastric juices are added while digestion begins in the third chamber. Large whales can process a great deal of food each day. The first and second stomachs of blue whales together can hold approximately one ton of food. While sperm whales pursue their prey in all oceans, baleen whales feed six months per year in high latitude waters that have plenty of food, then migrate toward the tropics. A large portion of the food is transformed into blubber that provides thermal protection in cold areas. It also provides the energy needed to migrate to mating grounds, whose warm waters are favorable for whale calves, but poor in food.

Reproduction, social life

Whales become sexually mature at 5 to 10

20

A gray whale's penis outside of the longitudinal groove in which it is kept most of the time.

years for baleen whales and a bit later for sperm whales. They can reproduce every two or three years and reach an average age of 30 years. The single offspring normally leaves its mother's womb tail first, which limits the chances of drowning, as it can be pushed toward the surface as soon as its head appears. Although whale calves are the largest babies in the world—a blue whale weighs 2.5 tons at birth—their gestation period is only 12 months for the baleen whales and 16 months for sperm whales. The baby comes into the world with all of its senses developed. The only things still missing are teeth or baleen plates, depending on the suborder to which it belongs.

From the time the baby is born, the mother's teats, under the pressure of milk, come out of the grooves in which they normally stay. The nourishing liquid is literally injected into the baby's mouth at nursing, which takes place under water, and must be interrupted each time the calf has to breathe at the surface. During the nursing period, the largest whales produce 150 gallons (600 L) of milk every day. Their milk, along with that of the polar bear, is one of the richest. It contains more than 40 percent fat (human milk only contains 2 percent). Due to this concentration, the mother limits her use of water while the baby doubles in size during its first week. Females take great care of their offspring, closely watching them until weaning and remaining ready to protect them until the next pregnancy.

The social life of whales is difficult to understand, because acoustic communication and the physical characteristics of their environment enable them to remain in contact at great distances. As a result, an individual that seems to be traveling alone may very well be part of a group whose members are simply far apart from each other. A 20-Hz sound, commonly produced by baleen whales, is perfectly audible 46 miles (75 km) away and still is, under certain circumstances, at more than 500 miles (311 km). Emitted with enough power, the sound should even be audible at nearly 6,200 miles (10,000 km), if it is not disturbed by the noise of ships that now cross all oceans. Whatever the case may be, it is certain that whales are very social animals.

Females, in particular, assist at births, while among some baleen whales a close collaboration between males to help one of them win a female has been observed. The homosexuality documented in small-toothed whales has also been observed in several species of big whales, specifically among right whales and gray whales. It seems mainly to involve young, sexually mature males that have not yet had the opportunity to impregnate a female.

Finally, play occupies a large part of a whale's time, among both young and old, and it sometimes includes the use of objects. Thus, it has been possible to observe, on numerous occasions, both baleen whales and sperm whales playing with tree trunks and clumps of algae.

21

The pattern of callosities on a right whale's head is different for each animal.

Parasites and companions

Like all animals, whales involuntarily carry internal parasites, in particular, various types of worms that live in their digestive system, liver, sinus, and auditory canals. But the most spectacular are external. Different kinds of barnacles, cirripedes, crustaceans, and other species that usually attach themselves to rocks and shellfish, literally embed themselves in a whale's skin. Transported by whales, especially the slowest (right whales, bowheads, gray whales), these barnacles feed on microplankton.

Other whale parasites, "whale lice," are not insects like their land-based counterparts but are also crustaceans, in this case from the family of cyamids. Like the lice on land mammals and birds, they firmly attach themselves to their host in order to suck their blood. While some cyamids are found in several species of whales, the majority have developed a species appropriate to each victim. So, for example, right whales, in the northern hemisphere, host the *Cyamus biscayensis*, while gray whales specifically host *Cyamus scammoni* and sperm whales

Nescyamus physeteri. Various species of phalarope follow baleen whales from time to time to remove some of these cyamids each time the whale surfaces.

Under water, whales sometimes have another companion, the remoras or pilot fish, which use the whales as a convenient form of transportation. They can be seen from time to time on the sides of sperm or fin whales that they don't harm. Neither do the veils of diatoms that can be found all over a whale's skin at certain times of the year harm the whale.

Predators

For several centuries, the principal predator of whales has incontestably been human. While gray whales and right whales have been hunted for a long time, man first began to hunt sperm whales in the 18th century, and all other species of whales in the 19th century, bringing them all, with the exception of the minke whale, to the point of extinction.

The only other predator worth noting is

22

A peaceful encounter between two killer whales and a humpback whale off the coast of the Antarctic peninsula.

another whale, the killer whale, which occasionally attacks whale calves or, attacking in a group, a single right whale. According to several studies carried out in the Antarctic area, the minke whale is the favorite dish of the killer whale.

Strandings

A whale stranding, which was certainly the first contact between humans and whales, is always a spectacular event. It was also, until recently, the only way for the general public to get close to these mysterious giants of the sea.

Sperm whale stranded in Oostduinkerke, on the Belgian coast, in February 1989. In December 1991, a sperm whale stranded on a sandbar nearby was able to free itself at high tide. However, four others were stranded and died together in the same area in November 1994.

Strandings happen for two reasons: the stranding of animals that die at sea and are carried to shore by wind and currents, and the stranding of live animals that seem to deliberately head for the coast. The first, which is less frequent, involves all species; it is a question of a decomposing body not eaten by scavengers before being pushed onto land. The second concerns certain toothed whales including the largest of them, the sperm whale. Sperm whale strandings are usually by males of the species that strand themselves, individually or in a group, an event that takes place regularly in certain low-lying shore areas with sandy bottoms

and strong waves, such as Cape Cod in the United States, or on the Belgian-Holland coast. On the Belgian-Holland coast, these have been regularly observed, at least since the 17th century, between the months of November and March. There is no definitive explanation for this behavior, which affects migratory animals, suggesting fatal navigation errors, the causes of which are not yet fully understood.

One explanation for live strandings, where whales swim onto shore, is that they make mistakes following the earth's magnetic field, which can change slightly due to local geographical properties and even temporarily by events like solar activity.

23

Principal differences between the two suborders of whales

TOOTHED WHALES	BALEEN WHALES
Single blowhole	Double blowhole
Teeth	Baleen plates
Asymmetrical skull	Symmetrical skull
Large brain	Relatively small-sized brain
Presence of a melon	Absence of a melon
Significant use of ultrasound	Significant use of infrasound
Peribular sinus well developed	Peribular sinus relatively less developed
Males larger than females	Males smaller than females
Long nursing period	Short nursing period
Strandings usually of live whales	Strandings of whales that died at sea

Hunting

People first became interested in whales when they used the mountains of meat and blubber from stranded whales.

In areas where there were plenty of whales close to the shore, people were no longer satisfied with waiting for a whale stranding. They began to slowly hunt them. The early hunters only had small boats and only hunted slow animals, such as right whales, or relatively small ones, such as gray whales. One of the oldest illustrations of this type of hunt was carved into a Siberian rock 3,000 years ago. In the same way, the Basques and Asturians pursued whales across Europe, at the end of the Middle Ages, before hunting them from Iceland and from Newfoundland at the beginning of the 16th century.

When whales became rarer off habitable coastlines, the small boats were transported by ship to hunt them on the high seas, farther and farther out. The English and the Dutch were the first to hire the Basques and to hunt bowhead whales off of Spitzberg because right whales had almost disappeared. Whalers from Denmark and Hamburg soon joined them. After several decades, whales were practically exterminated around the archipelago, and the hunt moved to more difficult areas, between Greenland and Baffin Island, where losses in ships and in lives were considerable. The best year for whaling in this area was 1820, when 688 whales were captured. However, ten years later in the same area the British whaling fleet experienced its greatest tragedy, losing 19 vessels at one time.

At the beginning of the 18th century, the Americans, who had participated under the British flag in North Atlantic whaling, were the first to go after the sperm whale, which is quicker. Setting off from the east coast of the United States, this kind of whaling, described by Herman Melville in *Moby Dick*, carried American whaling ships to all the oceans of the world up to the beginning of the 20th century. In order not to be dependent on land stations for preparing and melting blubber, whalers began to have brick ovens for preparing the oil on board, mounted on the middle of the bridge in their wooden ships. The days of sailing, and those of tens of thousands of whales, were numbered.

The first steam-powered whaling boat, which was British, appeared in 1857. Several years later, the Norwegians came up with the harpoon gun, which, with its explosive head, inflated whale carcasses, thus preventing them from bleeding. It was also the Norwegians who, in 1926, launched the first factory ship, which was sloped at the back so that whales could be hoisted onto the ship. According to the official figures, 27,000 whales were killed that year, reaching 55,000 on the eve of the Second World War. Later, when Antarctica had become the principal whaling region, all species of whales fell prey, in succession, to the seemingly unstoppable whalers. However, in 1946, the principal whaling nations joined together in the International Whaling Commission to preserve the supply of whales by limiting whale hunting. Nevertheless, the number of whales taken continued its nonstop increase, reaching the staggering figure of 64,680 reported catches for the 1964–1965 season. After this high point, the numbers tumbled, to no more than 5,000 in 1980.

In 1982, the Whaling Commission adopted a moratorium on commercial whaling that went into effect four years later. To get around this moratorium,

Originally hired by American whalers in the 19th century, today, sailors from Lembata continue to hunt sperm whale using traditional Indonesian boats.

26

Iceland, for several years, and especially Japan and Norway, continued to hunt several species under the pretext of scientific research.

France as a whaling nation

While the Basques were involved, beginning in 1610, in the early development of whale hunting by Holland, England, Denmark, and Hamburg, France had to wait for the creation of a special company by Cardinal Mazarin in 1644 to make its presence felt in whaling. French whalers were prevented by other whaling nations from establishing a base for melting blubber in Spitzberg. The French whalers developed stoves used for melting blubber on board ships. Despite this technical progress, and although it sent 20 whalers each year to hunt whales, the company went out of business in 1665.

With the disappearance of this privileged company, the return of the freedom to bear arms enabled other French companies to try their luck between 1669 and 1688. Some years, there were more than 40 whalers flying the French flag. Throughout the century, whaling involved the Basque ports of Bayonne and especially Saint-Jean-de-Luz.

Whaling was reinvigorated in France after the reign of Louis XIV. The number of whalers increased from 8 in 1712 to 30 between 1728 and 1733, then dropped until 1744, when the English hunted their last whale. There were some individual hunters until 1766, the year that marked the end of whaling from the Basque country.

The entry by the French into the American Revolution inaugurated a new era with the installation at Dunkerque of a group of American whalers originally from Nantucket. They renewed whaling, this time also hunting sperm whales. In all, the catch from ships at Dunkerque and Lorient reached approximately 500 sperm whales to 1,500 right whales between 1784 and 1793. Interrupted by the war with England, French whaling was briefly revived in 1802 to 1803, then had one final renaissance beginning in 1817, thanks to the help of the Americans. Ships sailed primarily from Le Havre but also from Bordeaux, Nantes, Dieppe, Saint-Malo, Lorient, Honfleur, and Marseille. The number of whalers was never more than 19 and France's whaling came to its final end in 1837.

Whale products

People hunted whales because they were economically very valuable. Until the advent of petroleum and electricity at the end of the 19th century, whales were coveted for their oil and their blubber, which were used in public and private lighting, and for manufacturing soap, wristwatches, and weapons. In the early 19th century, the trade in sperm whale oil became big business. The oil from the blubber and the spermaceti oil, from the head of the whales, became important to many industries. The standard candle of the time was made from spermaceti oil, and other products, such as shampoos and cosmetics, were made with whale oil. A mixture of oil from blubber and spermaceti oil was used to make germicides and detergents. In addition, sulfur could be added to it for use as a lubricant in high-pressure manufacturing, such as metal cutting and wiredrawing processes. Whale baleen were used in women's clothing, umbrellas, and brushes, while the ivory from the teeth of sperm whales was used in lots of ways. After these various products were

27

Cutting up a sperm whale in Iceland during the 1980s. This has now been suspended.

removed, the carcasses were thrown back into the sea. In the 20th century, all of the whale body parts became profitable and were transformed into concentrates of vitamin A, nitroglycerine, gelatin for photographic film, and nail polish. The best meat was reserved for human consumption (the rest ending up either in animal food or in fertilizer). Each year, some 300 minke whales are still killed in the North Atlantic by the Norwegians. The prime quality meat is sold in large supermarkets for about $53 a pound ($26 a kilo).

Today, unless you absolutely have to eat whale meat, there are substitutes available for all of the products taken from whales, often at a better price. One product that did not involve killing whales for it was ambergris. It is a waxy gray or brown substance that scientists believe is produced in the intestines of sperm whales, possibly in reaction to a pathogen. The whales expel the substance, which floats until someone finds it or it washes ashore. It has a very strong musky smell and was valued for its use in cooking and in making scented soaps and perfumes. At the time of its use, it was worth its weight in gold, but now there are many synthetic alternatives.

The Japanese and whales

Heirs to a centuries-old tradition of whale hunting, the Japanese respond poorly to international pressures—which they feel have been imposed on them by Europeans and Americans—designed to get them to give up whaling. While they continue whaling under the false pretext of scientific research, the Japanese have nevertheless become aware of the ecological danger inherent in the disappearance of whales. At the moment, whale meat hardly ever appears on Japanese menus, and customers are not exactly lining up in Tokyo's only restaurant still serving it as a specialty (and which takes great care to explain that it is from minke whales and that this species is not endangered). An obvious sign of this slow disaffection in a country where the law of the marketplace rules—whale sashimi costs no more in this restaurant than a good fish sashimi.

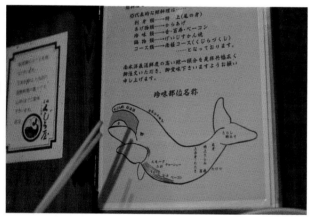

Whale sashimi in a Japanese restaurant. The menu specifies from what part of the animal the meat comes from—blubber, tongue, red meat, intestine, etc.

Pollution

Whales accumulate chemical pollutants that people throw into the sea. The pollutants become concentrated at each level of the food chain. This has been confirmed by analysis of their tissue, which specifically reveals important traces of organic synthesis products, such as DDT and PCB, along with heavy metals such as lead, mercury, and cadmium. The concentrations of pollutants are particularly high in the very young because some of these products become trapped in blubber, and enter their bodies via their mother's milk. Today, the impact of these pollutants on the health and fertility of whales remains unknown. Black tides and oil spills (extremely harmful to animals with fur) seem to have little effect on whales. On the other hand, drifting and lost nets create serious problems for both small and large whales, causing injuries, and even resulting in drowning.

Tourism

Whale-watching is a new form of encounter between humans and whales, one that is much more positive for whales. Started in California in 1955, it only included gray whales. It has slowly expanded to other regions of the United States, and then to Canada and Mexico in the 1970s. Beginning in the 1980s, this form of ecological tourism experienced considerable growth, on the order of 10 percent a year. While it is particularly focused on large whales, people have also become interested in smaller whales, as long as it can be predicted when these whales will be visible. According to the most reliable estimates, more than 5 million people have approached whales in 50 countries and in 15 overseas territories and dependencies, including Antarctica. This new pastime has led some Norwegian and even some Japanese whalers to no longer hunt but to whale-watch instead. This may, in time, save the whales.

29

Right whale near the coast of the Nuevo Gulf (Valdés Peninsula in Argentina). Only a few trip organizers with licenses can approach whales.

Gray Whales
(Eschrichtius robustus)
FRENCH: baleine grise
SPANISH: ballena gris

Description

Average length: male 43 ft (maximum 50 ft); female 41 ft (maximum 49 ft); newborn 15 ft
Average weight: adult 26 tons; newborn 1,500 lb.

It is mainly gray, spotted with white marks due to pigmentation, external parasites, and scars.

The gray whale does not have a dorsal fin. Instead it has a series of 6 to 12 "humps" on its back, on the end third of its body, beginning with a prominent hump.

A gray whale's skin, like the skin of a bowhead whale, is covered by lots of barnacles.

32

A gray whale sifting the bottom for food. It picks up sediment in its mouth, which is filtered as the whale rises up toward the surface.

Behavior

The gray whale is one of the most demonstrative whales. Visible in numerous locations and in varying circumstances, it offers watchers a large range of behaviors. It sometimes exhibits an obvious interest for the boats that get close to it. It likes to jump out of the water, emerging vertically, and falling back in on its side. It often lays on its side at the surface and flaps its flippers.

It can also lift its head above the surface, a behavior known as "spy-hopping."

Vocalization

The gray whale does not appear to be very loquacious but occasionally produces short moans between 20 and 20,000 Hz, which include a series of "clicks" ranging from 400 to 1,400 Hz as well as pulsed signals from 12,000 to 30,000 Hz, which are perhaps a form of echolocation.

Traveling

Its cruising speed is 2 mph to 5 mph (3.2 to 8 km/h), and it can move up to 14 mph (22.4 km/h).

Migration

The whales of the North American West migrate across large distances, traveling more than 5,000 miles (9,600 km) on each trip. From April to October, they feed in the Bering Strait and the Chukchi Sea.

33

From October to February, they migrate south, crossing the string of Aleutian Islands at the very beginning of winter, as far up as Unimak. Pregnant females go first, followed by the younger, nonpregnant females and the adult males. Sometimes late whales are caught in the early winter ice. Whales swim along the North American coast to return to their breeding grounds in Mexico's Baja California.

From February to July, the large group of whales begin to swim back north. Whales return in two waves. Beginning in February, the newly pregnant females leave, followed by juveniles, and males. In May, the females accompanied by their young are the last to leave. The migration takes place close to the coast, from bay to bay, with gatherings in several estuaries. During this period, the young begin to modify their feeding habits by supplementing mother's milk with marine organisms.

On the Pacific west coast, whales migrate from Korea up to the shores of the Sea of Okhotsk and Kamchatka.

Diving

Average depth 118 feet (36 m), with a maximum of about 500 feet (150 m); length of dives is between 3 to 5 minutes, with a maximum of 15 minutes.

Feeding

Unlike other large whales, the gray whale eats invertebrate benthic amphipodes (*Amplisca eschrichti, Amplisca macrocephala, Atylus carcinatus*) that it catches by filtering silt. It digs furrows at the bottom of the Bering Strait, working the sea bottom like a plow.

Resting on its side, it sucks in the sand. On the surface, it expels the water and the mineral deposits through the baleen plates, leaving behind a cloudy trail.

Life span

The lifespan of a gray whale is between 30 and 40 years, but may even be up to 60 years.

Reproduction

The mating season is between December and April.

Females give birth to a single baby every two years. The births take place at the end of the migration in shallow lagoons, extremely close to the shore.

The calf is darker than its

34

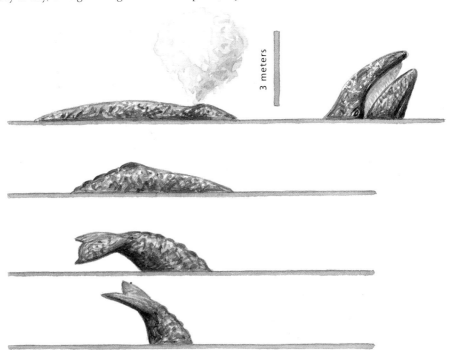

3 meters

mother and stays close to her during the first three months. It drinks 50 gallons (190 L) of milk and its weight goes up 67 pounds (30.4 kg) every day.

Distribution

Two separate populations live in the northern Pacific. One, in the west, has greatly suffered from whaling along the coasts of Japan and Kamchatka. The other group, in the east, migrates twice a year between Mexico and the Bering Strait. A third group used to live in the northern Atlantic, but they are now extinct.

Population

Having been brought to the brink of extinction, the population in the eastern Pacific is now estimated at 17,000 to 24,000 whales.

The group on the Pacific west coast (Korea) travels along the Japanese coast twice a year and has suffered from Japanese whaling. It seems that a small group of a few hundred whales has survived.

History

The northern Atlantic population of whales was too close to Europe and the large North American colonies, and was unable to withstand Basque, Norwegian, and American whalers. The last whale died toward the end of the 19th century.

The Pacific groups were hunted for a long time by coastal populations. Their predictable migration route was an opportunity for feasting for those with the courage to face them.

In 1845, whalers discovered the breeding ground of the east coast group. The whales were hunted there, and, in a few decades, the species was brought to the brink of extinction. Whaling Captain Charles Scammon hunted whales tirelessly. However, he left a collection of observations unique in their richness and precision of information for posterity.

Since 1946, gray whales have fortunately been totally protected, which has enabled their population to grow, at a rate of 2.5 percent per year.

35

Each year, gray whales are caught in the ice floe trap. In 1988, the warming of relations between the Soviet Union and the United States led to a huge operation to save two gray whales using technical means and the media.

Area of distribution.

Observation sites

Sea of Cortez, Baja California, Mexico

Gray whales can be found in the lagoons of Baja California where they mate. Baja California is ideal for newborn whales. The bays are shallow and, because of high salt levels, the water is very dense, which provides excellent buoyancy.

The first pregnant females generally arrive at the shallow lagoons at the end of January. Several days later, each gives birth to a single calf. At the same time, fully mature adults mate in the waves of the Pacific, not far from the coast. The mating period can also begin around November, during the winter migration.

Three deep bays cut into the peninsula's Pacific coast. Magdalena Bay in the south has mangrove-fringed lagoons. It is a remote bay about halfway down the Pacific side of

36

Mexico's Baja Peninsula. Dozens of gray whales have been observed there on any given day during the calving season. Moving north, Ballenas Bay is linked to San Ignacio lagoon by a channel. One hundred eighteen miles north of there, Eugenia point blocks the coast. It marks the entrance to Sebastian Vizcaino Bay, named after the Spanish navigator who explored it in 1602. This huge bay is broken up into three lagoons: Manuela, Guerrero Negro, and the famous Ojo de Liebre (Eye of the Hare) lagoon, better known to us as Scammon Bay. At the bay's exit, sharks and killer whales lie in wait for whale calves.

In this region, it is easy to see the typical behaviors that are characteristic of gray whales, such as "spy-hopping," which gray whales do to see what is happening at the water's surface. The whale holds itself straight up for a number of seconds using the back and forth movement of its tail. Its face is completely out of the water, 6 to 10 feet (2 to 3 m) above the surface. Sometimes they jump so high that nearly their entire body is out of the water. They can do two, three, four, or even five of these leaps in a row.

After coming up to the surface several times to breathe, they turn to dive by lifting their tail out of the water. This long, deep dive can last several minutes.

Blue whales, Bryde's whales, and fin whales can be seen in the Sea of Cortez. Minke whales, humpback whales, killer whales, and dolphin, are also common. So, too, are sperm whales, sei whales, pygmy sperm whales, pilot whales, and dolphins

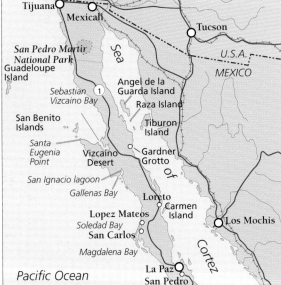

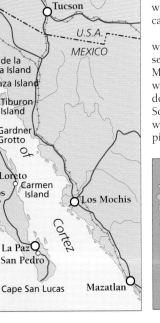

such as Risso's, spotted, spinner, and Pacific white-sided that also visit the area. California sea lions, fur seals from Guadeloupe, and northern elephant seals also frequent the area.

As of February, off San Benito Island, you can see enormous dominant male elephant seals fight for their territories. Guadeloupe Island, located several miles from the peninsula, is home to the largest northern colony of sea elephants and an endemic species of fur seal.

Baja California is a strip of land, 750 miles (1,200 km) long and 12 to 125 miles (20 to 200 km) wide between the Pacific and the Sea of Cortez (or Bay of California). Its southern tip is Cape San Lucas, a majestic promontory, jagged from the continuous beating of the Pacific Ocean.

The peninsula was created by volcanic eruptions. It is located on the San Andreas fault, which causes frequent earthquakes in San Francisco and Los Angeles. The peninsula is made of granite. It split from the rest of the continent 4.5 million years ago, and since then it has moved almost 310 miles (500 km) away. The Sea of Cortez was created by the gap between the continent and the peninsula.

The coast along the Sea of Cortez is sprinkled with lots of islands, large and small. The waters of Carmen Island are worth an underwater visit. Raza Island has a wonderful refuge that holds a variety of birds: brown pelicans, English puffins, dwarf petrels, black petrels, wheatear petrels, double-plumed cormorants, Audubon gulls, Hermann gulls, royal tern, elegant tern, American oyster catcher, Marbled Godwit, and blue-footed booby, to name only a few. Other islands are equally remarkable, such as Angel de la Guarda with its pelican colonies and elephant trees, Tiburon with its wealth of invertebrate marine life, and San Pedro Martir with its bird sanctuary and seal paradise. Some sites are particularly good for whale-watching such as the whale strait between the peninsula and Angel de la Guarda Island. The whale strait is extremely rich in zoo plankton and mainly attracts fin whales.

This abundance of marine life is due to the Colorado River. It deposits into the sea

37

Gray whale in water that is unusually clear. As whales move through shallow waters, sediment rises and the water becomes murky.

The prickly pear is one of many cacti unique to Baja California. It can grow up to 6 feet (1.83 m) high.

all the nutrients it accumulated on its 1,400-mile (2,250-km) trip to the sea. The bays of the Pacific coast have mangrove borders that are sometimes several miles.

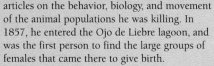

Flora and fauna

The peninsula's interior is a mineral desert, arid and mountainous. The rare rainstorms are violent and cut deep ravines into the ground. The rain and the wind erode the barren rocks. The violent rain storms that sweep through the area are called *chubascos*. The rainy season is between May and October, while winter and spring are the mildest seasons.

Despite its dryness, the Vizcaino Desert is rich in flora that has adapted to desert conditions. In the desert, plant sizes move from one extreme to the other, either tiny or gigantic. The most remarkable plants are the cacti. The enormous cactus uses all of the resources of the arid zones and has diversified into 350 different forms. The werewolf tree (cirio or *boujeum* in Spanish) has stems that look like huge tentacles.

38   Charles Scammon (1825–1911)

This great navigator has become almost a legend in the world of hunting marine mammals. A real Captain Ahab, he crossed the seas of the world in search of whales, elephant seals, seals, and sea otters. His presence was felt particularly in the North Pacific where he decimated whale populations for 20 years to supply oil for California pioneers, for wars, and for industrial development.

This great sailor had an acute sense of observation that enabled him to write numerous articles on the behavior, biology, and movement of the animal populations he was killing. In 1857, he entered the Ojo de Liebre lagoon, and was the first person to find the large groups of females that came there to give birth.

Hunting whales could be dangerous. Females became angry when small boats came close to their calves, and they used all their force to smash the whalers. The gray whales were so dangerous that whalers called them *devil fish*.

An excellent draftsman, Scammon recorded on paper the details of his hunts, the weapons and instruments used, as well as anatomical drawings of the whale species he killed. These line drawings also describe Native American hunting methods, their boats, and their harpoons. Full of regret, Scammon wrote: "Constantly pursued along the California coast, these animals are in danger of extinction, unless the few survivors have fled to an unknown location in order to find refuge."

Another plant unique to the peninsula is the extravagant elephant tree (colpaguin or *torote* in Spanish), with thick, long branches that look like an elephant's trunk. The elephant tree is not very tall, rarely taller than 12 feet (4 m) high. However, its boughs can spread over 40 feet (12 m). For several weeks each year, between May and September, it is covered in pink or red flowers.

A number of animals, including the harlequin snake, the ringed lizard, and the giant scorpion, are also part of this desert ecosystem.

The birds are not to be outdone either. The most remarkable is the California roadrunner. Raptors are well represented by the buzzard, the prairie falcon, and the red-tailed buzzard.

Mammals specifically include endemic species of kangaroo rats that quench their thirst by nibbling on vegetation and that live in burrows that they dig. Their predators are coyotes and pumas.

Observation

There are all sorts of organized whale-watching cruises, from 89-foot (27-m) boats to kayaks, and even traditional boats called *pangas*, which can carry a single person, and up to four people. Whales can be found in the San Ignacio lagoon, Ojo de Liebre (Scammon Bay), Guerrero Negro (national park) and Soledad Bay, Whale Strait, and Magdalena Bay.

You see whales from different places along the Pacific coast. You must be extremely careful when you go whale-watching. Do not try to approach the whales, wait for them to approach you, and above all do not try to come between a mother and her calf. Small boats are not allowed to enter lagoons without authorization.

PRACTICAL INFORMATION

The best time to see gray whales in Baja California is definitely March.

39

TRANSPORTATION

■ **BY PLANE.** There are several options: via San Diego, which is 15 miles (25 km) from the Mexican border; flying from Los Angeles to Loreto (1 hour, 50 minutes); starting from the southern tip of the peninsula, via La Paz (2 hours, 15 minutes). Flights also depart from Tijuana. Longer and more costly, is the flight from La Paz via Mexico.

■ **BY BOAT.** You can get to Baja California by ferry departing from Los Mochis or Mazatlán. During the 17-hour trip there may be occasional sightings of whales and sea birds.

■ **BY CAR.** You can rent a car in La Paz (Mexico) or in San Diego, but you cannot cross the U.S.–Mexico border in a rental car. The northern entry into the peninsula can be made either from Tijuana or Mexicali, capital of the State of Northern Baja California.

Count on five days of driving between San Diego and Cape San Lucas via Route 1,

which winds its way down the peninsula from one coast to the other.

You can take a bus, but you need to have a lot of time, and you have to be able to speak Spanish.

The highway system is generally good on the main routes; secondary roads are sometimes difficult.

DISTANCES

San Diego to Cape San Lucas: 1,116 miles (1,800 km)
La Paz to San Carlos: 140 miles (230 km)
Loreto to La Paz: 220 miles (360 km)

ACCOMMODATIONS

It is cheaper to stay with local people in their homes or in the comfortable small hotels in Loreto and close to Magdalena Bay in San Carlos. With its endless beaches and endless sunshine, the peninsula attracts sun-worshipers and big game fishing (for swordfish and marlin, both threatened with

extinction in the Sea of Cortez).

CLIMATE

The weather is hot and dry all year round. Rain is rare (less than 10 inches [250 cm] a year), but rainstorms can be violent. So, do not forget sunscreen (with a high protection factor), sunglasses, a raincoat, and a sweatshirt.

SIGHTS

The history of the peninsula includes many Jesuit missions. They have their own museum in Loreto.

The Gardner Grotto, which is difficult to reach, is decorated with numerous rock paintings (made between 1000 and 1500) representing the fauna of Baja California, including a gray whale.

Observation Sites

Vancouver Island, British Columbia, Canada

This large island covers 367,200 square feet (34,000 km²), and is like a rampart protecting the brilliant city of Vancouver, the third largest city in Canada with a population of 1.7 million. The island is named after the man who explored the region in 1792. Victoria, which is the official capital of British Columbia, is located on the Island.

Vancouver Island is a special place for nature enthusiasts. The best area for observing whales is located on the west coast, in the area of Tofino and Ucluelet. Migrating gray whales are seen off the west coast of the island in late November as they travel to their wintering grounds in Mexican waters. They are more easily seen, however, in March and April during their return trip to the Arctic feeding grounds. There are approximately 40–50 gray whales, though, that halt their northerly migration at Vancouver Island. They remain during the summer to feed around the island instead of traveling into the Arctic.

The geology of the region is varied, with sedimentary, metamorphic, and crystalline rock. Most of the crystalline rock dates from the early Mesozoic or late Paleozoic.

40

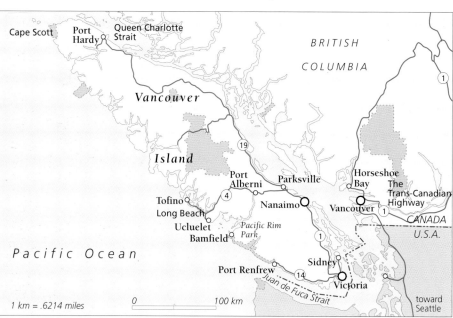

1 km = .6214 miles

Flora and fauna

This coast is one of the wildest in America, and has a number of attractions. The coast has been beaten by waves that have cut it into lots of deep fjords, small bays, and jagged cliffs. The cold waters are populated by a large diversity of animal life. During a boat trip you can see Steller sea lions and seals, as well as killer whales. Along the 19-mile (31-km) Long Beach, you can see buffaloes or bears that come at low tide to eat starfish, crabs, or mussels. In the pine trees, bald eagles lie in wait for salmon. The numerous streams are migratory routes for salmon that swim inland, sometimes dozens of miles, to mate. Other birds live on the shores and the cliffs: the Bachman oyster catcher, the belted kingfisher, the ruffle-tailed swallow, the red hummingbird, the Pacific gull, the harlequin duck, and the divers, to name a few.

The vegetation in these areas is particularly dense and diversified. The coastal forest consists mainly of four types of large trees: the hemlock (*Tsuga heterophylla*)

Bald eagles are a protected species and can now be seen in many places.

41

At low tide, the Pacific coast is full of plants and animals.

and the red cedar (*Thuya plicata*) are the main inland species; while the Sitka pine (*Picea sitchensis*) and the Douglas (*Pseudotsuga menziesii*) live along the coast. Wet clearings are covered in shrubs (bunch berry, salmon berry, thimbleberry, blackberry, huckleberry) and ferns. The flowers of the Castille brush, the white strawberry, and the Bermuda are particularly colorful.

The swamp areas are ideal for mushrooms, orchids, and carnivorous plants (droséra) to grow in. The rocky coasts are home to lots of algae that have adapted to difficult conditions, such as the sea palm, which can be seen at low tide. It can be difficult to observe the flora and fauna living on the jagged and slippery rocks, but just under low-tide height are kelp communities. Kelp is a type of algae, or seaweed, and when it grows extensively in one area it creates an underwater forest that many animals inhabit.

Observation

During the gray whale's annual migration, you can see it near Canada's west coast. Your chances of seeing gray whales here are not as good as in Baja California because only a small number of whales stop at Canada's west coast. Most of the group merely passes along the coast. The best whale-watching sites are in the Pacific Rim National Park, to the west, which can be reached via Port Alberni. You have to walk over a number of paths that closely follow the sea to cross this small peninsula with its cut-out.

At the western tip, Tofino is the 0-mile point for the Trans-Canadian Highway, which crosses the country for 4,800 miles (7,750 km).

On the coast, the best places to see whales are Shooner Cove and Wichaninnish Bay, where naturalists provide binoculars and tours for visitors. From Comber beach, you can see whales and sea lions eat together. Other interesting sites are Quisitis Point, Wya Point, and Green Point, where 50 whales came to feed one summer. Also on

42

Native American whale hunters

From the Oregon coast to Yakutat Bay in Alaska, over more than 1,500 miles (2,500 km) of coast land, several Native American groups distinguished themselves by their ability to follow gray whales during their migration.

The Nootka, who live at the tip of the Olympic peninsula and on the west coast of Vancouver Island, are among them. Whale hunting was mainly done for food, but it also played a very important sociological and spiritual role in their lives.

Before leaving, hunters purified themselves

in order to be worthy of taking a whale's life. Baths, chants, and incantations were done to make sure there would be no accidents while hunting.

The men's feelings toward the whales were a mixture of respect, fear, and eagerness. When the first blows were heard off the coast, several small boats went to sea, each with eight men on board. The chief, situated in the front of his boat, would give the signal to attack by throwing his harpoon first. Once the whale had been killed, the hunters would bring the cadaver back to the village, keeping it afloat using floats made out of sea lion skin.

Further north, the Haida, who still occupy the Queen Charlotte Islands, were known for their ability to build boats capable of withstanding the heavy swells of the North Pacific. Constructed from centuries-old cedars, these boats were beautifully decorated with stylized pictures of the village's animal-totem, which was often a killer whale or a whale! These sailors were incredibly persistent. They would follow whales well beyond the horizon, even though their only weapons were their paddles, their physical strength, and their war chants.

the west side of the island are South Beach, which is at the end of South Beach Trail, near Wickaninnish Center; Box Island, which is accessible from Schooner Trail; Portland Point; and Cox Point. In this area there is a good selection of trails from less than a mile to two miles in length.

In March and April, organized cruises follow the whales during their migration north.

In July, a six-day hike on the West Coast Trail, which links Port Renfrew with Bamfield, passes alongside coastal promontories where you have a very good chance of seeing whales.

Small boats (inflatable boats or kayaks)

leave from Port Hardy, making it possible to visit the creeks and coves that attract whales.

Finally, some whales spend the summer near the Island of Vancouver between Victoria and Cape Scott to feed on plankton. The Queen Charlotte islands are another good place to see gray whales. Vancouver Island has winters that are wet and cold and summers that are usually dry and warm. From September to May the southerly winds can bring rain and instant gales. In the summer, the mornings are often foggy and winds pick up in the afternoon. The best weather for viewing occurs in the summer when the whales are most abundant.

PRACTICAL INFORMATION

Boats make it easy to go to Vancouver Island if you are visiting British Columbia.

TRANSPORTATION

■ **BY BOAT.** The ferry leaves from Horseshoe Bay, northwest of Vancouver.

Departing from Washington state, a ferry links Anacortes to Sidney, in the southern part of the island, by crossing the Juan de Fuca Strait.

The time it takes on boat trips:
Port Hardy to Prince Rupert: 18 hours
Vancouver to Nanaimo: 1 hour 30 minutes.
Seattle to Victoria: 4 hours 15 minutes.
Travel on the island:
■ **BY PLANE.** There are planes between Vancouver and Tofino.
■ **BY CAR.** You can rent a car in Victoria or Nanaimo, both of which are linked to the Canadian mainland by ferry. There are fewer rental cars available at Port Hardy, which can be reached by boat from Alaska and Prince Rupert in the north.

There are only three highways on the island. Route 19 runs along the east coast, from Victoria to Port Hardy. Route 4 crosses the island from Parksville and Tofina. Route 14 runs along the Juan de Fuca Strait, in the southwestern part

of the island between Victoria and Port Renfrew.
■ **BY BUS.** Follow route 4.

DISTANCES
Victoria to Nanaimo: 71 miles (114 km)
Victoria to Tofino: 200 miles (325 km)
Nanaimo to Port Hardy: 250 miles (413 km)
Nanaimo to Ucluelet: 117 miles (189km)

ACCOMMODATIONS
Can be found in Tofino, at one of the three camping sites, or in hotels and bed and breakfasts; or in Ucluelet, in bed and breakfasts or motels (which are more expensive).

CLIMATE
Vancouver Island's west coast has mild and rainy weather. The average temperature for the driest month is 64°F (18°C). It rains a lot in winter but rarely snows. The average annual precipitation is 106 inches (2,700 mm).

SIGHTS
In Vancouver, the Anthropology Museum (Chancellor Boulevard, near the botanical gardens and the

university) has a remarkable collection of objects from northwest coast Native American tribes, as well as totem poles, a community house, and hunting canoes.

We recommend that you visit the Petroglyph park at Sproat Lake, between Parksville and Tofino. It is known for its prehistoric messages carved into stone. To complete your trip, do not miss a visit to the Whale Center (411 Campbell Street, Tofino, British Columbia), which retraces the history of the relationship between people and whales in this region. On exhibit are collections of tools and objects used by Native Americans, whalers, and settlers.

The Wickaninnish Center (Ucluelet, British Columbia) also provides information and offers you the chance to see the Pacific Rim National Park. Each year, Native Americans celebrate the whales' return to the north. For the occasion, a number of artists come together for the Pacific Rim Whale Festival.

43

Minke whales

(Balaenoptera acutorostrata)

OTHER NAMES: lesser rorqual, little piked whale
FRENCH: petit rorqual, baleine de minke, rorqual museau pointu
SPANISH: balena pequena, ballena minke

Description

Average length: from 26 to 30 feet (8 to 9 m) for adults.
Average weight: adult between 6 and 8 tons; newborn 77 lb (350 kg).

You can sometimes see the minke whale's flat, narrow head, along with the light gray grooves of its throat, when it comes to the surface. At the top of its head is a ridge that connects the blowholes at the tip of the snout. It has a white mark on its flippers.

Its blow is very diffuse and usually invisible. Its dorsal fin, in the shape of a "comma," is two-thirds of the way down on its back. You can see it each time a whale arches as it emerges from the water. When the whale is at the surface and about to dive, you can see both the blowhole and the dorsal fin.

Behavior

Minke whales often travel in small groups of three to five whales. Sometimes, when there is plenty of food, more of them travel together. The minke whale is curious and

46

3 meters

Minke whales mating.

often approaches boats and seems to want to come up close for a better look. It may make several close passes, then disappear. It can jump out of the water. It shoots up at a right angle from the surface, then falls flat. You rarely see the tail flukes.

Traveling

Its cruising speed is fast, around 16 mph (25 km/h).

Migration

Minke whales don't migrate on a regular basis. Minke whales are more abundant in summer only at the highest latitudes and return south during the winter.

Some groups appear sedentary.

Vocalizations

They can be classified as two types: muffled groans of low frequency and a series of "clicks" at higher frequencies.

Diving

We don't know how deep minke whales dive. We do know that although most dives last an average of 5 minutes, they can exceed 20 minutes.

Feeding

Their diet is rather eclectic. It consists mainly of small-sized fish that live in schools (anchovies, herring), but in

47

polar waters it also includes plankton. In the Antarctic region, the minke whale's diet consists almost exclusively of krill. In search of food, minke whales swim the closest to the polar ice than any baleen whale.

Longevity

40 to 50 years.

Reproduction

Mating probably takes place in February or in August. The time between 2 births by the same female can be as little as 18 months. After 10 months of gestation, the female gives birth to a single calf weighing 1,000 pounds (450 kg). It stays with its mother for 6 months.

48

Distribution

Minke whales can be seen in all the seas of the world, from the coasts of Antarctica to the edge of the Arctic ice field. They are, however, more common in cold waters than in the tropics.

Population

At the moment, the minke whale is the most common rorqual and may be the most abundant whale, with a population of between 500,000 and 1 million whales.

History

For a long time, rorquals were beyond the reach of

harpoons because they traveled so fast. With the advent of modern techniques, this has changed. Hunters attacked the largest of the rorquals, the blue whale, first, then the fin whale, and then the minke whale, which is much smaller and thinner. It is the only whale that is still officially hunted.

Possible Confusion

It is possible to confuse the minke whale with Bryde's whale, the sei whale, the fin whale, and the northern bottlenose whale.

Minke whale under water. You can see its tapered shape, characteristic of all rorquals, and its relatively large dorsal fin.

Blue whales

(Balaenoptera musculus)

FRENCH: baleine bleue, rorqual bleu
SPANISH: Ballena azul

Description

Average length: male 82 ft (25 m) (maximum 102 ft [31 m]); female 85 ft (26 m) (maximum 108 ft [33 m]); newborn 23 ft (7 m)
Average weight: between 80 and 144 tons (maximum 178 tons); newborn 2.5 tons.

Blue whales are the biggest whales. Their bodies are completely blue-gray with a large light-colored mark that goes from their chin to the middle of their stomach. This mark can vary in color, from yellow to white, as it is caused by unicellular algae. The blow is vertical and almost 30 feet high (9 m). The head is long and marked by a medial ridge that ends at the blowholes. The dorsal fin marks the rear quarter of the animal. Having a triangular or hooked shape, it is a good point of reference to identify the species as it is small in relation to the rest of the animal (12 inches [30 cm]). The flippers are relatively short. The tail is visible only when the animal dives

49

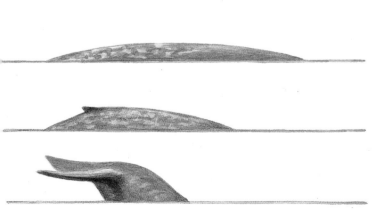

3 meters

3 meters

50

deeply. When the tail appears, it immediately plunges into the water at a right angle.

Behavior

Blue whales are not very demonstrative. Only the young jump, without their bodies entirely leaving the water. The blue whale travels in small groups of three or four.

Traveling

Its cruising speed is rather high, reaching 7 to 9 mph (11.2 to 13.4 km/h). In flight, it can move 18 mph, because its tail is up to 23 feet wide (7 m).

Migration

The blue whale migrates every year across large distances. In the summer, when the pack ice disappears, it comes to feed in the Arctic or southern regions. In winter, it lives below the equator, in subtropical zones, and does not seem to eat.

Vocalizations

The blue whale produces repeated groans in infrasonic vibration, between 12.5 and 200 Hz, as well as pulsating sounds in the 21,000- to 31,000-Hz band, which might be used to pinpoint schools of krill. It can be extremely noisy. Off the coast of Chile, a recording was made of a blue whale's whistle at a strength of 188 decibels, much louder than an airplane when it takes off.

Diving

Average depth of approximately 500 feet (150 m); duration is between 2 and 20 minutes.

Feeding

The blue whale feeds selectively. Its diet basically consists of planktonic crustaceans living in compact schools and moving upward during the night. Blue whales feed at the beginning and the end of the night at a depth of at least 130 feet (40 m). During the feeding period, a blue whale can ingest 4 tons of krill a day. In some regions, it also eats small fish, living in schools, such as sardines.

Longevity

More than 80 years.

Reproduction

This species lives in couples or in small groups of three individuals. For whales that feed in the Saint Lawrence River, births take place in tropical waters around Costa Rica, after a 12-month gestation period. A baby whale drinks 158 gallons of milk a day. Suckling lasts 7 to 8 months.

Distribution

Blue whales live in all the world's oceans, from . Antarctic waters to the edge of ice fields in the Arctic.

Population

It is very difficult to estimate the size of the blue whale population. It probably includes between 6,000 and 14,000 whales.

History

The blue whale suffered from the development of modern whaling techniques. The cannon-fired harpoon and the factory ship decimated it to the point that, in the 1960s, there were some cries of alarm announcing the imminent disappearance of the species.

Its population, estimated at 300,000 whales in the 19th century, was killed in the 1930s at the rate of several thousand per year. Protected since 1967, the population currently appears to be showing signs of growth.

51

Observation sites

The whale route, Quebec, Canada

The Saint Lawrence River is a vital communication route for both Canada and northeastern United States. Europeans first entered the North American continent traveling up this river. Today, it plays an important economic role because of the heavyweight ships that travel on it. But the Saint Lawrence is above all a river that is unique in its size and in the links between its waters and that of the Atlantic Ocean.

Formed only a few thousand years ago, the river ended up in a deep groove that separates the Gaspé Peninsula from the Canadian mainland, a continental mass that remained buried under icecaps for thousands of years.

From its outlet at Lake Ontario to the Island of Orleans downriver from Quebec, a distance of 310 miles (500 km), it is as wide as a river. Then its waters mix with those of

the ocean, and the Saint Lawrence River has tides. The Quebecois call it a sea. The river ends in the Saint Lawrence Gulf.

The waters of the Saint Lawrence are home to a large number of seals, whales, and birds. The reason for this profusion of life is the sudden rising of cold water from the Arctic. This cold current moves along the Labrador coast and reaches a continental heel, created by Anticosti Island on one side and the mouth of the Saguenay on the other. When the cold Arctic water rises into the warmer surface water, it brings nutrients from deeper regions. This is called upwelling. The single-celled algae at the surface and seaweed growing in shallow water use these nutrients to flourish and, as a consequence, become the basis for a rich food web. Then the current rushes into the river's calm waters.

Opposite Anticosti Island, the Mingan Archipelago is made of 40 islands, large and small, protected by the province of Quebec since 1983. Made of limestone, the coasts of the islands have been sculpted by waves into huge shapes that look like animals or faces.

52

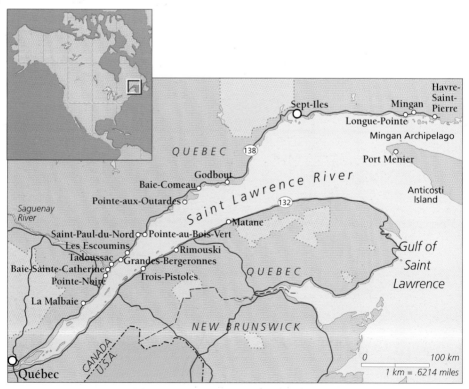

Flora and Fauna

On the route that leads to the whale-watching sites, at least three areas are worth a detour: Saint-Paul-du-Nord, Pointe-au-Bois-Vert, and the Pointe-aux-Outardes marshes, where a variety of water fauna takes refuge, primarily during migratory passages. The Pointe-aux-Outardes provincial park consists of eight different environments covering a one-half-square-mile (2.4-km) area, which include pine forests, dunes, and peat bogs, as well as the fourth largest marshlands in Quebec with 200 identified bird species. At Grandes-Bergeronnes, the bay at Bon-Désir park has lots of eiderdown ducks, and a colony of herring gulls.

If you are on the whale route in September, take the Trois-Pistoles ferry, a great way to see skuas, dovekies, phalaropes, and whales.

Colonies of marine birds, specifically monk puffins and black-legged kittiwakes, take up summer residence in the Mingan Archipelago. The loon and the Arctic tern, a species usually found in the Arctic as its name indicates, can also be seen there.

The flora of the Mingan Archipelago is also worth seeing. The vegetation, which includes the wonderful yellow cypripede, grows in the limestone soil. At each outlet to the sea, gray seals and eiderdown ducks can easily be seen.

Observation

Each summer, blue whales appear in the waters of the Saint Lawrence River, near the Mingan islands on the northern coast. They come to feed on amphipodal crustaceans. Tadoussac is located where the Saguenay runs into the Saint Lawrence, and is well known for whale-watching.

Never go out to sea without a naturalist on board, since you need correct information to whale-watch.

Along the Saguenay's south bank, the

53

There are lots of gray seals, but they are spread out throughout the North Atlantic from Scotland to Maine, and are easy to see at the mouth of the Saint Lawrence River.

Belugas are increasingly rare in the Saint Lawrence River, but they are flourishing in the Arctic.

54

winding route is beautiful, and is punctuated by several observation points. The Pointe-Noire "interpretive center" gives you information about whales and lets you watch them through a telescope.

To the north of Tadoussac, the Cape of Bon-Désir has promontories, close to the lighthouse, overlooking the deep waters of Grandes-Bergeronnes. Minke whales come very close to the shore here.

Moving further north, between Tadoussac and Baie-Sainte-Catherine, you might see one of the river's rare beluga whales.

This remaining group, trapped in the area during the last ice age, has very much suffered from the river's pollution and from intensive hunting by the riverside residents. Belugas, which are related to narwhals, grow to about 18 feet long. They are nicknamed "sea canary" because of the high trills and whistles that they make. The young are born gray but gradually lighten until they are white, like adults. In the Arctic belugas travel in large pods of 100 or more individuals, feeding in shallow water.

There are only about 100 belugas and you are not allowed to approach them. From here

The Basques

In the Bay of Biscay, from Biarritz to Bilbao, Basque seamen started hunting right whales in the 9th century, as illustrated on the seal of the city of Biarritz. Having decimated the coastal populations, they crossed the Atlantic. By the end of the 15th century, they had discovered on the Saint Lawrence coast, and particularly in the strait of Belle Isle that separates Newfoundland from the mainland, large populations of right whales.

From 1560 to 1570, whaling was in full swing for the five summer months. Lots of stations, housing thousands of men, were set up on the coast of Labrador at Middle Bay, Blanc-Sablon, and Red Bay, to name only a few locations. The Red Bay station produced almost 530,000 gallons (2 million L) and was manned each summer by a thousand men.

Originally from Saint-Jean-de-Luz or Bilbao, they braved the whales from their

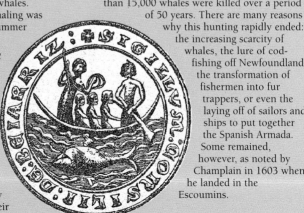

sloops, and were able to adapt their traditional techniques, which were too dangerous for the tumultuous waters of the Saint Lawrence. Instead of being pulled by the whale, they tired it out by attaching floats to the harpoon line. The whale carcass was then brought back to land to be dismembered. At the end of the season, galleons brought the precious cargo back to Europe. Historians estimate that more than 15,000 whales were killed over a period of 50 years. There are many reasons why this hunting rapidly ended: the increasing scarcity of whales, the lure of cod-fishing off Newfoundland, the transformation of fishermen into fur trappers, or even the laying off of sailors and ships to put together the Spanish Armada. Some remained, however, as noted by Champlain in 1603 when he landed in the Escoumins.

you may also see harbor porpoises, which are among the smallest cetaceans. They are usually less than 6 feet long and weigh about 100 pounds. The name "porpoise" apparently loosely came from "sea hog" in French. They swim in small pods up rivers and close to shore, feeding on small fish. They are often seen surfacing in shallow water near shores and boats.

For serious whale-watchers, the best solution is to go to Longue-Pointe and to go on a trip organized by the Mingans-Longue-Pointe Research Station. Richard Sears, who founded this organization in 1979 and is currently its director, knows each blue whale by name and can give you its family tree and its migratory route. His reference points for identification are not the white marks located on the tail, as they are for the humpback whale, but those on its back.

In Grandes-Bergeronnes, minke whales can easily be seen from the shore.

PRACTICAL INFORMATION

Be careful! During peak season, July–August, rates are higher and early reservations are a must.

55

TRANSPORTATION

■ **BY PLANE.** You can get to British Columbia by taking a direct flight from Montreal or Quebec, or with a stopover in Toronto.

You can then fly to Tadoussac, Sept-Iles, and Havre-Saint-Pierre from Montreal or Quebec.

■ **BY BOAT.** Several links are available between the banks of the Saint Lawrence: Rimouski to Sept-Iles, Matane to Godbout, Havre-Saint-Pierre to Port Menier (Anticosti Island), and Tadoussac to Baie-Sainte-Catherine. Boat crossings provide not only round-trip service, but also the chance to see marine mammals.

■ **BY CAR.** Route 138 follows the northern coast of the Saint Lawrence, from Quebec to Havre-Saint-Pierre, where it ends. From there, you will have to take the coastal expressway to reach the villages on the lower northern coast.

All of the major auto rental companies have offices in the airports of Montreal (Mirabelle or Dorval) or Quebec. Rentals are inexpensive and vehicles from major companies are generally in good condition. It is also possible to rent a car in Tadoussac, Sept-Iles, or Havre-Saint-Pierre.

■ **BY BUS.** This is by far the most economical method, with daily bus service between Sept-Iles and Montreal (15 hours) or Quebec (12 hours).

DISTANCES

Montreal to Quebec: 157 miles (253 km)
Baie Comeau to Sept-Iles: 142 miles (229 km)
Sept-Iles to Havre-Saint-Pierre: 136 miles (219 km)
Montreal to Havre-Saint-Pierre: 700 miles (1,125 km)

ACCOMMODATIONS

There is something in all price ranges, from camping (watch out for stinging insects in June and July) to better hotels. At least once you should try a bed and breakfast. They are comfortable, friendly, and ideal for sampling the cuisine of Quebec.

SIGHTS

In Tadoussac, a village dedicated to the whale, visit the marine mammal "interpretation center" opposite the port, created and directed by a dynamic, able team that is, among other things, working on the problems of whale survival (the work of Robert Michaud, in particular).

The interpretation centers in Havre-Saint-Pierre and Longue-Pointe organize seminars, films on nature, and trips to nearby islands. If you want to visit an Indian reservation, avoid Wendake outside of Quebec and instead try the village of Mingan where the Montagnais sell crustaceans they have caught. It is also the home of the Montagnaise Cultural Center.

Fin whales

(Balaenoptera physalus)

OTHER NAME: common whale
FRENCH: rorqual commun, grand rorqual
SPANISH: ballena fin

Description

Average length: male 69 ft (21 m); female 72 ft (22 m); newborn 20 to 21 feet (6 to 6.5 m). This is the second biggest whale.
Average weight: adult between 45 and 70 tons; newborn 2 tons.

A fin whale's head is pointed, in the shape of a V. Its back is usually dark gray, and its stomach is white. One of the characteristics of this species is the asymmetrical coloring of the jaws. On the right side, the white from the stomach reaches as far as the upper lip; on the left, the lower jaw is dark. The bottom of the fins and tail are white. A single blow can reach 20 feet high.

56

Behavior

After a dive, the fin whale appears, showing its narrow, tapered head and the light gray grooves of its throat. As it moves along the surface, the small dorsal, which is two-thirds of the way down its back, appears when the blowhole disappears. Among a school of fish on the water's surface, the gray whale swims with its head to the side. The blowhole disappears before the dorsal fin can be seen.

Fin whales like to live in groups. This large whale is the most gregarious. Groups in feeding areas can be made up of dozens of whales. Fin whales tend to follow their route without paying much attention to the boats, as long as they are not in their way.

Traveling

The fin whale, nicknamed the "greyhound of the seas," is the fastest whale. Its cruising speed is around 11 mph (18 km/h) but it reaches a top speed of 18 mph (28.8 km/h) and a surface speed of about 37 mph (60 km/h).

Migration

Fin whales usually migrate over large distances. Some whale groups go on seasonal trips covering more than 12,400 miles (20,000 km). These trips are not taken at the same time every year and do not follow clearly marked routes. Migration is normally between warm areas, used

Like all whales, the fin whale has only one baby at a time. This one is receiving very rich milk from its mother, which is literally injected into its throat each time the baby suckles.

for mating, and cold areas rich in food. Some groups appear sedentary or move only small distances, like fin whale groups in the Sea of Cortez and in the Mediterranean.

Vocalization

Fin whales seem to express themselves primarily in the 20- to 200-Hz band but they also produce "clicks" with a frequency that reaches 30,000 Hz.

Diving

Dives have been measured up to 650 feet (200 m) deep.

Feeding

Depending on the feeding site, they eat either krill or fish (sardines, herring), and, in the Mediterranean, zooplankton and mainly small crustaceans from the euphausiid family.

Longevity

Probably reach 100 years.

Reproduction

Mating takes place in the winter in tropical waters and births

occur the following year in the same areas. The baby drinks its mother's milk for the first six months of its life, doubling in size during this period.

Distribution

Fin whales live in all the seas of the world, from warm to polar waters, from the Arctic to the Antarctic. In the summer they can be seen in the Mediterranean between Corsica and the mainland, in the Ligurian Sea.

In spring, they migrate between Spain and the Balearic Islands. They can also be seen in the Bay of Biscay.

57

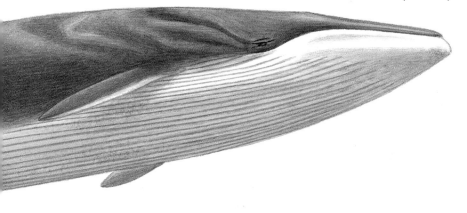

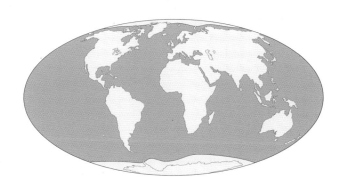

Population

It is always very difficult to estimate whale populations. The total number of fin whales may be in the area of 100,000 whales, an estimate that some consider optimistic.

History

For a long time it was out of the reach of hunters because it was so fast. It has been hunted since the advent of modern techniques.

Notes

Can be confused with the minke whale and the blue whale.

58

The fin whale's dorsal fin can only be seen when its head is under water.

The Ligurian Sea: France and Italy

The Ligurian Sea is part of the western Mediterranean. It extends from the coasts of Liguria (Italy) and Provence to the south of Corsica and north of the Balearic Islands.

A vast plain of regular relief, the Liguro-Provençal basin, with an average depth of 1.5 miles (2,500 m), is bordered by a steep continental slope. This steep ascent causes a phenomenon known as upwelling (the rising of cold, rich water from the depths toward the surface).

The average temperature in this area is 75°F (24°C) in summer, which is relatively cool for the Mediterranean.

The coast of Provence is the point of departure for whale-watching. It consists of two different geological areas. The first is made up of crystalline rock such as gneiss and granite, and includes the Massif de l'Estérel and the Hyères Islands. The other area is made up of sedimentary rock such as limestone and sandstone, and includes the Massif des Calanques, among other places.

Corsica and Sardinia, which were still close to modern-day Provence 28 million years ago, are now some distance away because of the movement of tectonic plates that created the Ligurian Sea.

Flora and fauna

A number of marine bird species are visible in the same areas as whales, and the first few hours of a whale-watching cruise can be devoted to ornithology. Attracted by the same food supplies, the common puffins and black guillemot follow the whales as they travel.

Along the coast or crossing the islands, you can see the light-colored swift and the

59

At sea, the presence of birds, such as puffins and shearwaters, can indicate the presence of one or several rorquals.

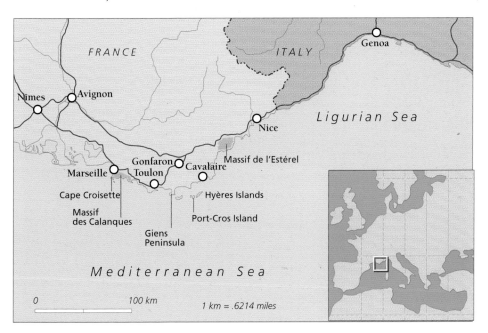

Audouin gull, and even the booted eagle and the Eleanor falcon. The Giens peninsula is a great place to see birds along a coast where birds are subject to numerous pollutants. Avocet and white-headed stilt nest in the Giens peninsula, while migratory birds, mainly sandpipers and ducks, go there in the spring.

Several species of Nordic marine birds spend the winter at sea in this area. Gannets, great skuas, Arctic skuas, and monk puffins are among the best known.

The flora of the Provençal coast reflects the two different kinds of geological environments. The Aleppo pine can take hold in the smallest crevices of the porphyry cliffs, while the cork oak and the holm oak are well rooted in the siliceous soil. People are moving into the scrub land in limestone areas. You can only see the stone breaker and the Marseille astragalus, typical Mediterranean species, in a few places, such as Cape Croisette near Marseille.

Aristotle, Pliny, and whales

Aristotle was probably the first known "cetologist" in history. In 350 B.C., he had already correctly separated fish from whales, and even differentiated between baleen whales and toothed whales. In Book VI of his *History of Animals*, he specifically wrote that "the whale and the other cetaceans, which have blowholes rather than gills, are viviparous...they produce an embryo which grows into a fetus, as it does in man... All animals with blowholes breathe and absorb air because they have lungs." He also notes that they "suckle their young and take them inside themselves while they are small."

This last bit of information probably comes from the fact that babies are born tail first and that their head stays inside the mother until the very last minute. However, most of Aristotle's observations are incredibly accurate.

Less systematic than Aristotle, whom he is pleased to contradict on several points, Pliny the Elder, in his *Natural History*, written in the first century A.D., adds some interesting descriptions to Aristotle's information. Pliny wrote that one of the largest animals in the Indian Ocean was the whale, while the biggest in the Sea of Gaul is the "blower that stands up straight like an enormous column and which, taller than the sails of ships, ejects a torrent of water." He describes, in great detail, how "the killer whales burst in on the whales' retreats, tearing apart with their teeth calves, or mothers who have just given birth, or females who are still pregnant."

Zoology was trapped in the Dark Ages for many centuries after Aristotle and Pliny. All Western scientists, relying on the *Book of Jonah*, considered whales to be fish. This biblical interpretation meant that whales could be eaten on Good Friday and during Lent. Whales continued to be grouped with fish until 1758 when the Swedish naturalist Carl von Linneus

hesitatingly placed them among mammals in the tenth edition of his *Systematic Classification of Nature*.

Sixteenth-century German engraving (J.-M. Dumont collection), showing sailors trying to push away an approaching humpback while a sperm whale has just blown on the other side of the ship. Lower down, a killer whale has caught a seal.

60

Observation

The minke whale population of the Liguro-Provençal basin is estimated to be about 1,000 whales.

Strandings by young whales along with genetic analyses show that these rorquals spend all of their lives in the Mediterranean. A number of minke whales have been seen near the Strait of Gibraltar, suggesting that some might swim out to the Atlantic. However, this is not considered to be a major migration.

The synthesis of 21 years of observation (Beaubrun's Synthesis, 1995) made it possible to identify two periods during which the minke whales are most abundant in this area: from April to May between Italy and Corsica, and from July to August between Corsica and the coast of Provence.

They feed along the continental slopes, where zooplankton is especially abundant.

Lots of toothed whales also come to this area. The sperm whale, the black pilot whale, and the Risso's dolphin like to swim in these deep areas (more than 3,280 feet [1,000 m] deep) where they can find their favorite food—squid. These species are present throughout the year in the Liguro-Provençal basin. If pilot whales are close, you may hear them bellow as they surface. Sailors used to imitate this bellow to attract whales. This calling of the whales was known as Caa'ing, and it has also become a nickname for the whales. The blue and white dolphin, the most common Mediterranean whale, can also be easily seen here, along with the common dolphin and the bottlenose.

Several organizations offer whale-watching trips from Toulon or Cavalaire. The trips are generally on sailing ships and last from three to seven days depending on which observation route you choose to take.

This is not a leisurely vacation. Most of the "training courses" are for motivated individuals who are ready to adapt to the requirements of life on board ship and the scientific goals of the organizers. Do not expect to become a whale expert in just one week. Your financial contribution, however, is always welcome since it goes to serious scientific research on whales.

61

PRACTICAL INFORMATION

In summer, the weather is usually good, with mild winds, warm temperatures, and clear skies.

TRANSPORTATION
■ BY PLANE. Several airports are located near whale-watching departure points: Toulon, Nice, Marseille. These places are about an hour's flight from Paris.

■ BY TRAIN. From Paris, the TGV goes to Marseille (in 4 hours and 30 minutes), as well as to Nice.

■ BY CAR. The Mediterranean coast is easy to get to, unless you are traveling during peak vacation time. Once you arrive at the port, you will have to park your car somewhere for a week.

DISTANCES
Paris to Nice: 688 miles (1,109 km)
Toulon to Nice: 100 miles (159 km)
Nice to Genoa (Italy): 96 miles (155 km)

Toulon to Ajaccio: 167 miles (270 km)

ACCOMMODATIONS
Since whale-watching trips go for several days, you live on board. Back on land, you have to make reservations at a hotel or campsite, especially if you are traveling in July or August.

CLIMATE
It is important to know the marine weather forecast for the areas of Genoa, West Corsica, and Provence since strong gusts of wind can rise up quickly. The Gulf of Genoa is an area where strong winds build up. One of these is the Libeccio, a warm west-northwest wind. Storms are rare but very intense.

SITES
Port-Cros Island has been a protected national park since 1963. You should really go to see it, both on land and in the sea.

With a mask, a snorkel, and a pair of flippers, you can see the rich animal and plant life along the shore: sea urchins, sea anemones, and scorpion fish.

A path weaves its way through vegetation typical of crystalline Provence: holm oak, euphorbia, and rose garlic. To get the most out of your walk, use a local guidebook. Do not forget that you are not allowed to pick any of the plants in the park.

The village of Tortues de Gonfaron (on route N 97) is dedicated to protecting, caring for, raising, and providing information on the Herman's tortoise—the only land tortoise in Provence.

Humpback
Whales

(Megaptera novaeangliae)
FRENCH: baleine à bosse, mégaptère, jubarte
SPANISH: yubarta, ballena jorobada

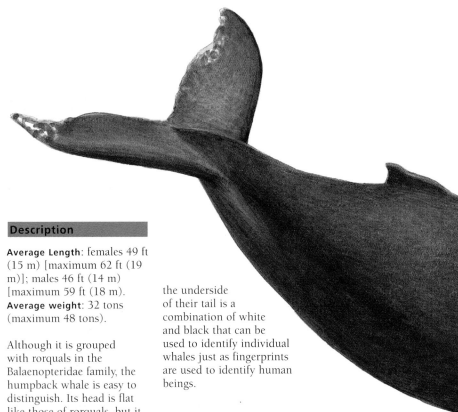

Description

Average Length: females 49 ft (15 m) [maximum 62 ft (19 m)]; males 46 ft (14 m) [maximum 59 ft (18 m).
Average weight: 32 tons (maximum 48 tons).

64

Although it is grouped with rorquals in the Balaenopteridae family, the humpback whale is easy to distinguish. Its head is flat like those of rorquals, but it is more rounded, and on the median line of the rostrum and around its mouth it has characteristic large bumps. Once past the head, the body quickly gets larger and becomes thickset. Their flippers are remarkably large, corresponding to one third of the whale's length. The shape of the dorsal fin varies from one individual to another. The tail is rounded in a crescent shape with ends that point toward the rear end of each of the two flukes. The tail has an indentation in the middle and jagged edges. Humpback whales are completely black on the top of their head and their back. Their flippers, stomach, and the underside of their tail is a combination of white and black that can be used to identify individual whales just as fingerprints are used to identify human beings.

Behavior

Of all the large whales, the humpback whale is certainly the most demonstrative, although we don't understand the meaning behind its behavior. Humpback whales often leap completely out of the water, even several times in a row. Swimming on their side, the whales sometimes slap the surface with a flipper or, stomach in the air, with both of them. They freely approach small boats and sometimes seem to play around them. They frequently scan the horizon, upright with head pointed toward the sky. They also

3 meters

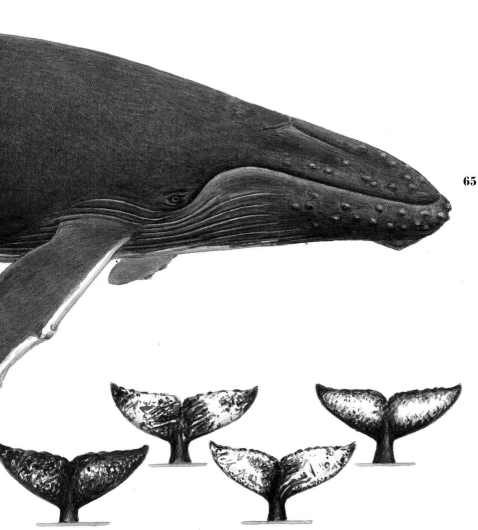

65

The coloring on the underside of the tail is different for each individual, making it possible to identify a humpback whale as surely as with a passport.

often use, either alone or in a group, a very specific fishing technique. They quietly swim up under a school of fish or krill, releasing a string of air bubbles, making tighter and tighter circles. The frightened prey gather in the center of the circle and are eaten by the whale(s) who emerge open-mouthed.

Traveling

During migration, the humpback swims at 6 mph; in flight faster than 16 mph.

Diving

66 The humpback whale can stay underwater for 30 minutes but often dives for much shorter periods of time, usually 5 to 10 minutes. It usually does not go down very deeply, probably not beyond 656 feet (200 m).

Vocalization

The humpback whale emits high frequency "clicks" reaching 30,000 Hz. It also produces, in frequencies between 20 and 9,000 Hz, songs that are the longest and the most varied in all the animal kingdom, with repeated sequences about 15 minutes long.

At the beginning of mating season, all the male humpback whales in a given area intone the same song, which evolves up until the end of winter. The whales stop singing when they leave the warm waters. The following year, when it is once again mating season, they pick up where they left off at the end of the previous season. Sightings in the clear waters of the Hawaiian Islands have shown that the males sing only when they are alone and when they assume a specific posture:

while diving at a depth of 20 feet (6.1 m), with their bodies at a right angle. Most of the time, whales do not release bubbles while singing.

Migration

The humpback whale begins its migration at a fixed time every year along well-established paths between the subpolar regions where it feeds and the tropical coastal areas where it reproduces during the winter.

When winter ends, the pregnant females are the first to leave for the feeding grounds, followed by the males. Females accompanied by their young are the last to leave the warm waters. At the end of summer, it is the males that are first to reach the tropical seas while, once again, the females, accompanied by their young, complete the journey.

Feeding

When they are in cold waters with an abundant food supply, the humpback whale eats 2 tons of fish and planktonic crustaceans a day, in two to four meals. It prefers to feed on fish in the Northern Hemisphere and almost exclusively on krill in the Southern.

Longevity

The life expectancy of a humpback whale is estimated to be around 40 years.

Reproduction

Gestation lasts for one year. At birth, the calf measures

3 meters

approximately 16 feet (5 m) and weighs 2,980 lb. (1,350 kg). Its mother nurses it for 11 months. During this period, a male frequently accompanies a female and her calf in order to protect them, but it is not yet known whether this means that the male is the calf's father.

Distribution

There are humpback whales in every ocean. In the Northern Hemisphere, the two Northern Atlantic groups migrate, one from Norway to Cape Verde, the other from Newfoundland to Bermuda, while the largest of the four Northern Pacific groups spends the summer off Alaska and the winter in Hawaii.

Population

Protected internationally since 1966, the world population of humpback whales has been increasing gradually. They fact that they are not dangerous and that they follow very precise migration routes makes it easy to see them, but the humpback whale is rare. Today, it is estimated that there are only 6,000 of them.

History

Of all the balaenopterids, the humpback has the largest amount of blubber in proportion to its size. On top of that, its natural

curiosity pushes it toward ships, so humpback whales have been vigorously hunted since the end of the 19th century.

At a distance, it may be confused with the fin whale, but as it dives, the humpback whale's tail is out of the water, while that of the fin whale is not.

67

Having surrounded a school of fish in a circle of bubbles, these humpback whales simply take a mouthful.

Atlantic Ocean, New England

If you look at a map of New England, or if you fly over the ocean between Newfoundland and New York, at the same level as Boston, you will see a strange strip of sand that extends into the sea and folds back on itself: this is Cape Cod, so named because of the abundance of cod that surrounds it. This strange peninsula, 68 miles (110 km) long, which became an island after a canal was built to shorten the trip between Boston and New York, is in fact a part of the frontal moraine abandoned by the enormous glaciers that covered the North American continent during the first ice age.

The cradle of American history, New England is also the cradle of sperm whale hunting, a type of whaling that took place far from its shores and that sent American whalers out to all the oceans of the world.

Flora and fauna

In Maine, mainly around Bar Harbor and Northeast Harbor, you can see lots of harbor seals. Gray seals are also found there, but only around Mount Desert Island and in Flanders Bay. You can easily see a number of marine birds, such as the northern fulmar, the gannet, skuas, great skuas, and phalaropes, as well as Arctic terns that spend the summer in the dunes of the Cape and in those of Plymouth Harbor (between Cape Cod and Boston).

In the lagoons of Cape Cod, horseshoe crabs (*Xiphosura polyphemus*) proliferate, especially during the month of May, when they come by the thousands to mate.

This strange animal, which is about 24 inches (60 cm) long, is related to the trilobites that lived in the seas during prehistoric times, and has remained intact through many eras. Despite its exterior resemblance to crabs, this arthropod belongs to a specific class, that of the chelicerates, midway between crustaceans and spiders.

68

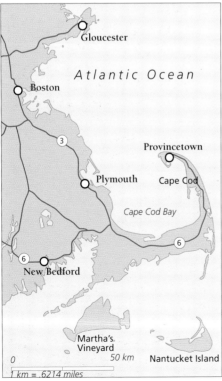

Horseshoe crabs arrive in large numbers to mate on the beaches of Massachusetts.

Observation

While sperm whales are rarely seen in New England waters, these waters are a haven for those who want to see the many baleen whales that come to stay there at different times of the year.

In particular, it is an ideal location for easily getting close to the humpback whale, from mid-April to mid-October, in one of their feeding areas.

Observation boats leave from several points along the coast, from Montauk in the south—on Long Island, New York—to Bar Harbor, Maine, in the north. Kennebunkport, Gloucester, Boston, and Plymouth are all good departure points, but we particularly recommend Provincetown, at the end of Cape Cod, Massachusetts.

After the humpback whale, the fin whale is the most frequently sighted large whale in the area, and from time to time it is also possible to see minke whales. In April, occasional right whales with their calves pass as they return from the warm waters of Florida and Bermuda to their winter feeding

69

Native Americans, whales, colonists, and sperm whales

Whales that had died at sea, including sperm whales, were frequently stranded in the Cape Cod area and nearby islands (Martha's Vineyard and Nantucket) because of currents and sandbars. Their carcasses were a precious source of food for the Native American tribes in the area.

Occasionally, when whales would approach the shore or enter a bay, the Native Americans would force the issue by chasing them in their small boats and killing them, as told in 1605 by the British Captain George Waymouth. The first European colonists also took advantage of the remains brought in by the sea and, beginning in the 1620s, began to hunt the large whales, following the example of the Native Americans.

In the mid-17th century, many small, newly created companies chartered larger ships to hunt. They mainly hunted right whales, which were slow and fat, until 1712

when Captain Christopher Hussey successfully hunted a sperm whale. Until that time, these animals had been made use of only when they were stranded naturally, but their oil was much more precious and sought-after than that of right whales. This is how the hunting of sperm whales began. It quickly moved to areas far from these coasts, and sent American whalers out to all the oceans of the world. It considerably enriched Nantucket, and then New Bedford, and played an important role in the development of Boston and New York up until the advent of petroleum.

In Mystic, on the bridge of the *Charles W. Morgan*, there are stoves for melting blubber.

grounds further north.
Off the coast of New
England, humpback whales
are frequently accompanied
by common dolphins and
Atlantic white-sided dolphins.
During observation trips, you
can sometimes see seals on
their own or pilot whales in
groups. Both of these animals
are nomads that do not return
to New England regularly
each year. Another interesting
ocean nomad is the basking
shark. This shark, which can
grow to 30 feet or more, feeds
by swimming with its mouth
open to strain plankton out of
the water. It swims near the
surface and can occasionally
be seen during whale watch
trips in New England waters.
The sight of a 20–30 foot
shark with mouth gaping is a
wonderful addition to whale sightings.

Established by the descendants of Portuguese sailors who had
been hired by American whalers, the Dolphin Fleet, departing
from Provincetown, offers you the chance to get close to many
species of whales.

70

PRACTICAL INFORMATION

The best time to see the humpback whale off the coast of New England
is from mid-April to mid-October.

TRANSPORTATION
■ **BY PLANE.** From Boston,
there are regular flights to
Provincetown.
■ **BY BOAT.** There are regular
trips between Boston and
Provincetown.
■ **BY CAR.** The roads are
excellent.
■ **BY BUS.** Boston and New York
are linked to Provincetown by
very comfortable buses.

DISTANCES
Provincetown to Boston: 115
miles (185 km)
Provincetown to New Bedford:
93 miles (150 km)
New York to New Bedford: 208
miles (335 km)
New York to Boston: 217 miles
(350 km)

ACCOMMODATIONS
There are two well-equipped
campsites in Provincetown as
well as a large selection of
hotels in all price ranges.

SITES
All of the area between New
York and Boston is marked by
whaling, which, unintentionally,
contributed to the development
of this area up until the advent
of petroleum. If you are
interested in this saga, you
must visit New Bedford and its
Whaling Museum, incontestably
the most beautiful in the
world.
In Mystic Seaport, in
Connecticut, the village and
the 18th-century port have
been restored. You can board
the last of the American
whalers, the three-masted
Charles W. Morgan, built in
1841 and decommissioned in
1928. The museum also has
exhibits associated with a
whaling town. There are shops
depicting the making and
selling of goods, such as
barrels, sails, and iron works.
Also, ships had to have
functioning time pieces,

compasses, and instruments
like sextants to properly
navigate the oceans. The
museum has a large collection
of these. During the summer
season, you may encounter
someone "in character" such as
a whaling boat captain or
perhaps a sailor dancing a jig.
The island of Nantucket,
which was, from the mid-18th
century to the American
Revolution, the most important
whaling port in the world prior
to being supplanted by New
Bedford, is also worth visiting.
It also has an interesting
museum, located in a factory
where candles made from
sperm whale oil were
manufactured. Another
museum worth visiting is
located in Bar Harbor, Maine,
in northern New England. For
those staying in New York, visit
the American Museum of
Natural History, where large
whales have a prominent place.

Island of Maui, Hawaii

The Hawaiian archipelago extends across the Tropic of Cancer in a narrow line of 1,670 miles (2,700 km). It is oriented from northwest to southeast, in the middle of the Pacific Ocean. The fact that the islands are clearly larger toward the east, where there are active volcanoes, and are therefore the newest islands, gives you a hint as to how the islands were formed. The islands were formed when the tectonic plate slid on what is called the global hot spot. The oldest island, Kure, formed 35 million years ago, is slowly sinking at the western end of the archipelago, while in the east another island is rising from the waves. Maui, made up of two volcanoes rising from the ocean floor situated 3.3 miles (5,400 m) below, was one of the last to rise up. It is, above all, the island of whales.

The interior of the island of Maui is covered with lush vegetation that is watered by numerous waterfalls and streams.

71

Flora and fauna

In the archipelago you may also see another marine mammal, the Hawaiian monk seal. Shy and solitary, its total population is made up of no more than 1,600 seals.

The fauna of Maui, along with that of the rest of the archipelago, suffered greatly from the arrival of man some 1,500 years ago and

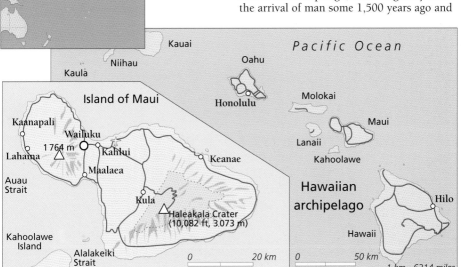

Kauai

Niihau

Kaula

Oahu

Pacific Ocean

Island of Maui

Honolulu

Molokai

Kaanapali

Wailuku

Maui

1764 m   Kahului

Lanaii

Lahaina

Keanae

Kahoolawe

Maalaea

Auau Strait

Kula

Hawaiian archipelago

Hilo

Haleakala Crater (10,082 ft, 3,073 m)

Kahoolawe Island

Hawaii

Alalakeiki Strait

0   20 km   0   50 km

1 km=.6214 miles

The powerful waves of the Pacific Ocean have cut into and sculpted the volcanic rock, creating lots of spaces for the island's luxurious vegetation to grow.

72

How sperm whales helped make Hawaii an American state

Colonized approximately 1,500 years ago by the Polynesians, the archipelago of Hawaii was visited by Spanish galleons between the second half of the 16th century and its "discovery" by Cook in 1778.

Various elements support this thesis, specifically a Spanish map captured by the British in 1742 and the presence in Hawaii of helmets, capes, and arms manufactured locally, but unknown in neighboring islands, and that are very much like those used on Spanish ships in the 16th and 17th centuries. For whatever reason, the islands were barely touched by European civilization until the arrival, around 1820, of the first New England whalers.

During the mid 19th century, the ports of Honolulu and Lahaina made the archipelago a central point in

the North American whaling industry. Several hundred ships stopped there each year, en route to or returning from hunting expeditions for sperm whales throughout the Pacific or for right whales in the extreme north of the Pacific Ocean.

While the oil was sent to the United States, the ivory from sperm whale teeth made its way to the Asian markets, particularly China.

Increasingly integrated into the American economy, Hawaii was annexed by the United States in 1898 and became a state in 1959.

This pendant is made up of a carved sperm whale tooth held in place by a lock of hair (Museum of Man collection).

from competition with newly introduced species. Dozens of plants and animals that evolved here in extreme isolation have disappeared, most significantly 20 kinds of flightless birds that were easy for people to hunt. However, the island still has several native birds, of which the best-known is the Hawaiian goose or nene. It was saved from extinction and is now the state bird of Hawaii. It lives inland, in areas of average altitude.

Despite the damage caused by wild pigs, plants fared fairly well from the massive introduction of new plants. Naturalists will be fascinated by the diversity of plant life, and there are a number of botanical gardens.

PRACTICAL INFORMATION

The best time of year to see humpback whales in Maui is from December 15 to April 15.

TRANSPORTATION

■ **BY PLANE.** While Honolulu is the main port of entry into Hawaii, Maui is also directly linked by plane to several major American cities. Traveling by plane is also the most practical way of moving between islands because there are no regular connections by ship.

The Maui airport is located in Kahului, on the island's northern coast, 15 miles (24 km) from Lahaina. The city is one hour away from Honolulu.

Once there, boats are available for excursions, but not for transportation.

■ **BY CAR.** Maui has a good network of roads. Taxis are practical for short distances but can quickly become very expensive.

■ **BY BUS.** There is a bus system on the island.

DISTANCES

Honolulu to Kahului (Maui): 100 miles (160 km)
Kahului to Lahaina: 15 miles (24 km)

ACCOMMODATIONS

Maui has all sorts of hotels, youth hostels, bed and breakfasts, and campgrounds. You should make reservations well in advance.

CLIMATE

From December to May, the temperatures range from 65 to 86°F (18 to 30°C).

You will need a sweater for cool evenings, and a thick sweater and windbreaker for climbing Haleakala. The temperature in Haleakala can range from 50 to –6°F (10 to –20°C).

SITES

In Lahaina, some of which is the same as it was in the 19th century, do not miss visiting the *Carthaginian II* floating museum, a two-masted square-rigger with an exhibit on the age of whaling. It shows an excellent documentary on the humpback whale.

In Kaanapali, 3 miles (5 km) to the north of Lahaina, the Whalers Village Museum (free admission), in the Whalers Village Shopping Complex, retraces Hawaii's whaling past. It also has a complete sperm whale skeleton on view.

Besides whales, Maui has a considerable number of attractions, particularly for those interested in flora and in geology.

The Kahului Botanical Gardens provide a good introduction to plants, which can be completed at the Keanae Arboretum, 16 miles (26 km) east of there. Situated halfway up the side of the Haleakala volcano (10,000 ft [3,055 m]), the Kula Botanical Gardens offer an excellent sampling of higher altitude plants, while Silversword Garden is an excellent resting spot at 8,900 ft (2,700 m) on your climb to the top of the volcano. The top of the volcano is impressive, for its plants—it crosses seven climate zones—and its geology. All of the area surrounding the summit is part of the huge Haleakala natural park, which has over 31 miles (50 km) of marked trails. You must stay on the trails in order to preserve the very fragile flora at this altitude.

The naturalist should not leave the Hawaiian islands without visiting the most eastern and the most recent of the islands, the Big Island, 31 miles (50 km) east of Maui. In the Hawaii Volcanoes National Park, you can get close to constantly active volcanoes. An unforgettable sight!

73

Among the most remarkable vegetation is the silversword (*Argyroxiphium sandivicense*), a native species that grows only in Haleakala. This high-altitude plant usually grows in isolation on the red ash, forming, over the course of 10 to 20 years, a tapering ball of silver-gray leaves. From this 3-foot-high (1-m) sphere, a floral shaft grows to a height of almost 8 feet (2.5 m), with its orange flowers blooming for several weeks before the plant dies.

Humpback whales in Maalaea Bay.

74

Observation

It is estimated that there are approximately 1,500 humpback whales still living in the north Pacific, or one-tenth the number that existed at the beginning of the century. More than 500 of them come to mate and to spend the winter around the Hawaiian islands, particularly in the strait that separates the island of Maui from that of Lanai. They start to arrive in late October and the last ones leave the archipelago's waters in early June.

Lahaina, today a simple small town on the southwest coast of Maui, was the capital of the Hawaiian islands before Honolulu became the capital in the mid-19th century. Lahaina was, from 1819, and for more than 40 years after, the main stopover for American whalers hunting sperm whale in the Pacific.

Today, whale lovers go there to see another species, which was of no interest to the whalers of that time—the humpback whale. It winters in Hawaiian waters, mates, and gives birth to its young there.

It is here that most of the recordings were made of the famous whale songs, which greatly contributed to the protection of the species. In 1992, a law enacted by Congress created the Hawaiian Islands Humpback Whale National Marine Sanctuary off the archipelago to promote observation of the humpback whale and scientific research related to it.

In addition to organized boat excursions departing from Lahaina, you can see whales from several points along the coast. The best-known place is located 9 miles (14 km) southeast of Lahaina, at the entry to Maalaea. The view is superb on Maalaea Bay, dominated by the Haleakala volcano, but it is also one of the few places on land where it is possible to see humpback whales accompanied by their young.

Three smaller whales can also be frequently seen around Hawaii: the bottlenose dolphin, the pilot whale, and the false killer whale.

Observation Sites

The Antarctic Peninsula

The Antarctic Peninsula is a spit of land that escapes from the enormous Antarctic continental mass and that points toward South America.

Antarctica is in fact a tectonic plate that became detached from Gondwana, the continental mass that included Africa, Australia, India, South America, and Antarctica, and that began to migrate south about 200 million years ago. These movements are responsible for the formation of a mountain range along the axis of the peninsula, in continuation of the Andes cordillera. The highest peak is 10,000 feet (3,050 m) high.

The movement of the Antarctic and South American plates in opposite directions formed an arc that is clearly visible thanks to the emerging islands of South Georgia, the South Orcade Islands, and the South

Sandwich Islands, that were once in line with the Andes cordillera and the peninsula.

The peninsula is made up of volcanic rock in the west and sedimentary rock in the east. From 600 to 40 million years old, the sedimentary rock contains traces of luxuriant vegetation and many animals (fish, reptiles, and invertebrates) that lived on this land when it was located in latitudes with a more favorable climate. The entire continent began to be covered with ice approximately 25 million years ago to form a glacier, an ice cap several miles thick.

At the same time that tectonic plate movements separated the two continental plates, a cold circumantarctic current formed a hydrological barrier around the continent. The current circulates in a clockwise direction and comes up against the peninsula where part of this current moves in the opposite direction forming a loop. This phenomenon is responsible for a resurgence of rich, cold water, the ideal environment for an explosion of life.

75

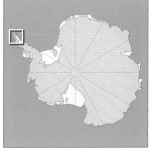

Norwegian whalers

The Norwegians are great whale hunters and are used to hostile conditions. They have been hunting minke whales for food since the middle ages. Whales that ventured into the fjords and became trapped were shot with arrows. In the 19th century, the trapped whales were shot with rifles. The hunting of minkes, belugas, pilot whales and bottlenose dolphins along the shore lasted for many years. Norwegians also sailed into distant waters in search of larger and more profitable whales. They came in large numbers to hunt rorquals in the Antarctic waters. Equipped with a cannon-launched harpoon invented by one of their countrymen, Sven Foyn, they established several bases for whale hunting.

At the beginning of the 20th century, they established in South Georgia Island the Grytviken whaling station, the first of a series of six. The last ceased operations in the early 1960s. The installations have remained in place, with equipment for melting and storing blubber. Factories for making harpoon heads show what methods they used for whale hunting.

During the 1929–1930 season, about 40 English and Norwegian factory ships, accompanied by 200 hunting boats, crossed Antarctic waters. The overproduction that followed caused the market to crash and required the establishment of quotas.

Deception Island was the home of one of these stations, occupied by the Norwegians until 1931 (the peak year for factory ships). This island, which is part of the South Shetland archipelago, is in fact a volcano. It is a caldera that sank several dozen yards (meters) in the southeast, enabling the sea to come in. This narrow fault, bordered by cliffs, forms a natural bridge. Ships entered this immense circle to take shelter in Whaler's Bay.

The French explorer Jean-Baptiste Charcot stopped there to take on a fresh supply of coal from the Norwegians. He noted that the water in the bay was so warm that it removed paint from the ships.

Despite repeated eruptions, there are still the ruins of bases, furnaces, and cisterns for visitors to see.

Many skeletons of large whales still litter the beaches of nearby islands in Port Lockroy or in Port Circumcision.

In summer, which is January in the Southern Hemisphere, humpback whales are abundant along the Antarctic Peninsula free from its straight jacket of ice. In the distance, peaks, many that people have never climbed, are over 5,000 feet (1,524 m) high, dug out by innumerable glaciers.

PRACTICAL INFORMATION

Don't forget that Antarctica is an ecological sanctuary.

TRANSPORTATION

■ **BY PLANE.** You fly into the city of Ushuaia.

DISTANCES

Ushuaia to King George's Island (Arctowski base): approximately 50 hours by cruise ship; 6 days by sailing ship (on average).
Deception Island to Petermann Island: approximately one day by cruise ship (depending on ice conditions and the ship).

ACCOMMODATIONS

In Ushuaia, lots of hotels welcome tourists leaving for the peninsula. On the peninsula itself, accommo-dation is on board the ship.

CLIMATE

The climate in the western part of the peninsula is relatively stable. In January, which is mid-summer in Antarctica, the temperature does not go above 41°F (5°C); in winter it only rarely reaches –6°F (–20°C).
  Rough storms can develop in a few hours due to the catabatic winds created by the phenomenon of evaporation on the surface of glaciers.
  Precipitation is light, but it can snow in mid-summer. In the Beagle Canal, it rains a lot in all seasons.

SITES

Bases can be visited in different places. Chilean, Ukrainian, or American, they are mainly for scientific and meteorological research, but they sometimes fill the function of souvenir stores.
  On Petermann Island, at Port Circumcision, a mound of stones stands as a reminder to the wintering of the *Pourquoi-Pas?* (Why-Not?), the polar exploration ship captained by Jean-Baptiste Charcot in 1909.
  In Ushuaia, the End-of-the-World Museum has many photographs of Fuegian populations, which have now disappeared.
  The Fire Ground National Park is made up of several biotopes—marshlands, rivers, rocky coasts, and beech forests. This environmental richness attracts many species of bird such as the burrowing owl, the crested caracara, and the Magellan woodpecker.

At the northern tip of this current, cold, dense water mixes with warmer, less dense waters coming from the Atlantic, Pacific, and Indian Oceans. This interaction is called Antarctic convergence. When you cross this area in a boat, you can feel the air temperature change within a few miles, and you start to see different kind of birds.

Flora and fauna

No land-based macro-fauna has developed on the Antarctic continent since its isolation and cooling down 30 million years ago.

The animal population basically consists of marine animals, the best known being the penguin and the pinniped. The most common species are the gentoo, Adelie, and chinstrap penguin.

In the midst of penguins busy raising their young, you can sometimes see a couple of macaroni penguins and an occasional imperial cormorant. The Emperor penguin visits Antarctica during some of the coldest

In January, chinstrap penguin chicks are already big. Well fed by their parents, they leave the land starting in March, before winter begins again.

78

On the beaches, like this one in Cuverville, the Antarctic fur seal and gentoo penguins pay no attention to each other, each going about its own business.

months of the year. These 4-foot, 90-pound birds leave the ice and waddle a couple of miles onto the Antarctic ice to rear their young. Once they have reached their destination, the female lays an egg, gives it to the mate and departs, only to return when the chick hatches. The male remains to incubate the egg and to provide the first meal. He regurgitates food he has saved in his stomach for those two months.

The Antarctic fur seal, one of the 17 species of seals in the world, is in a period of expansion, forming larger and larger groups. After being at the brink of extinction in the late 18th century, it now benefits from the increased scarcity of filtering whales, a competing species that also eat krill.

Three species of seal populate the waters of the peninsula and neighboring islands: the Wedell's seal, the leopard seal or sea leopard, and the crab-eating seal.

Plants barely develop in these southern latitudes. Only a few mosses and numerous lichens have been able to adapt themselves to the rigors of the climate. You must not walk on top of these slow-growing plants.

Observation

Many species of whales arrive during the southern summer to feed off the Antarctic coast. They include sperm whales, right whales, fin whales, blue whales, and humpback whales. It is estimated that at the beginning of the century they numbered 1.1 million and annually consumed 190 million tons of krill. Statistics on whaling estimate that 1.3 million whales were killed between 1920 and the late 1960s.

Leaving the tropics where they mate, humpback whales travel along the South American coast to feed in Antarctic waters on more than 1,100 pounds (500 kg) of small crustaceans a day. Sperm whales are abundant in the many bays and straits, as they prefer to feed above the continental shelf, while other baleen whales, present at this time in the vicinity of the peninsula, prefer to remain at sea. Often in pairs, with a mother always accompanying her young, they remain on the surface and barely move. They are not very timid and large boats can get close to them without danger. Sometimes they come up several feet from an inflatable dinghy or a sail boat.

Leaving from Ushuaia, you may see a minke whale or a fin whale, or even a group of Commerson's dolphins. You can also see killer whales crossing between icebergs searching for a seal or a group of penguins.

79

Paradise Bay in the summer sun is an amazing spectacle. Tightly enclosed, it provides convenient shelter for two scientific and tourist bases, as well as lots of crab-eating seals.

Right Whales

Right Whale

(Eubalaena glacialis)

OTHER NAMES: great right whale
FRENCH: baleine franche noire,
baleine de Biscaya, baleine des
Basques
SPANISH: ballena franca

Description

Description: Average length:
male 98 ft (14.5 m); female
52 ft (16 m) (maximum 59 ft
[18 m] for both sexes);
newborn 15 to 23 feet
(4.5 to 7 m).
Average weight: 54 tons
(maximum 96 tons);
newborn 1 ton.

Right whales are black. They
have light colored callosities
on their heads, around their
eyes, and on their chins.
Callosities that are grouped
together on the edge of the
snout are called a "bonnet."
These callosities are used to
identify each whale. A white
mark in the middle of the
stomach is another way of
identifying a right whale, as
well as the fact that it does
not have a dorsal fin. Its
flippers are short. Its head is
30 percent of its body.
   A right whale has a blow
that is in a clearly visible V
shape reaching 16 feet high
(5 m).

Behavior

Right whales are fairly
demonstrative. These placid

82

Progression in formation of a
herd of right whale.

whales often do a series of jumps out of the water. Another typical behavior is slapping the water's surface with a flipper. This large slap can be heard on the surface almost half a mile (1 km) away.

A right whale often lifts its flippers or holds its tail very high up above the water. Right whales are very playful. They even play with tree trunks. Mother and calf often play together.

Vocalization

The sounds produced range from 160 to 2500 Hz.

Traveling

The right whale travels slowly. Its cruising speed is 6 mph (9 km/h). Its maximum speed is no more than 10 mph (17 km/h).

Observations have shown that this whale sometimes

Blow in the form of a V characteristic of right whales.

83

3 meters

uses the surface of its tail, spread out widely, as a sail.

Migration

Right whales make two major migrations between feeding areas, located in polar or subpolar regions, and mating sites, characterized by shallow, relatively warm waters. They need at least one month to travel between the feeding area and the mating site, a distance of about 3,100 miles (5,000 km).

Diving

At sea, average depth: 990 feet (300 m); length between 10 to 20 minutes maximum.
Off the coast, dives last between four to eight minutes.

Feeding

A right whale's diet consists exclusively of small crustaceans that it filters through its particularly long (8.5 feet [2.6 m]) baleen plates. During the feeding period, it can eat from 1 to 2.5 tons of food per day.
The southern population feeds in subantarctic waters. Its principal prey is krill (*Euphausia superba*).
One of the methods used by right whales to feed consists of six or seven coming together at once and swimming in a V formation. They move on the surface at a constant speed, the mouth open wide in order to hold the crustaceans on their baleen plates.

Longevity

The lifespan of right whales averages 50 years.

Reproduction

Mating takes place in spring. This is a period of great excitement in whale groups, with several males pursuing a single receptive female. Gestation lasts 9 to 10 months. Females give birth to a single calf in shallow waters. It will be suckled for one year and will remain at its mother's side for another two or three years.

Distribution

There are two distinct populations that are some-times separated into two species: *Euballena australis* in the south and *Euballena glacialis* in the north. *Euballena glacialis* is made up of three clearly distinct groups. One group is in the North Atlantic, and travels between the Gulf of Mexico and Greenland. The second group is in the North Pacific, and travels along the coast from Mexico to Alaska. The final group lives in the Bering Sea and the Sea of Okhotsk.
The population in the Southern Hemisphere occupies a band ranging from 30° to 65° latitude south of the equator. The third group

84

3 meters

can be seen in South Africa, New Zealand, Argentina, and Southern Australia.

Population

The world population is estimated at between 2,000 and 3,000 whales, of which 500 live in Australian waters. The North Atlantic group is made up of 350 whales.

History

The name right whale comes from the fact that it does not sink when it is harpooned, which made it a good whale for hunters. This trait meant that it was hunted by the earliest European whalers, who were Basques.

At the end of the first millennium, there were many whalers in the Bay of Biscay.

Since the end of the 15th century, they have had to venture as far as the shores of Labrador to pursue the right whale.

In Australia and in New Zealand, more than 25,000 right whales were killed between 1827 and 1930, and the species was at the point of extinction.

Fortunately, protective measures, established in 1935, enabled their population to increase little by little.

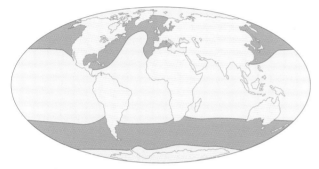

Leap executed by a right whale as observed from an Australian cliff.

85

Observation Sites

Nullarbor Coast and Eyre's Peninsula, South Australia

Eyre's Peninsula is named after Edward John Eyre who, in 1839, explored this wild area on foot and on horseback. This corner of land, which sank into the ocean, is bordered in the. east by Spencer's Gulf and in the west by the Great Australian Bight. Its furthest tip, Cape Carnot, is made up of the oldest rocks in Australia, dating from two billion years ago. It is crossed by a route with an evocative name: the Whaler's route.

The region that is most interesting for whale-watchers is the coast of the Great Australian Bight. The dunes of Bunda Cliffs climb 295 feet (90 m) above sea level and herald the great semiarid Nullarbor Plain, which means a place "where there are no trees."

A red kangaroo carrying her baby in her pouch. Ranging from 6 to 6.5 feet (1.8 to 2 m) high, it is the largest existing kangaroo.

86

Flora and fauna

The semiarid Nullarbor, while it does not have a single tree, is covered from May to November by multicolored flowers: ephemeral daisies and sturt's desert pea, to name a couple. In this region, 368 species of

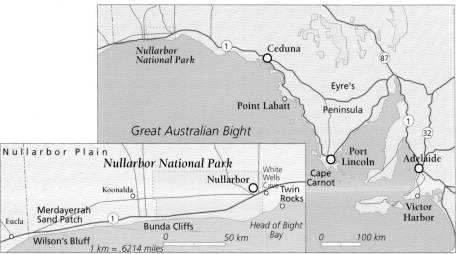

This 8-inch-long (20 cm) pine cone lizard is trying to frighten the photographer.

The only easily observable continental colony of sea lions is located at Point Labatt. The little blue penguin also lives in this area, but since it is an endangered species, we think that it is inappropriate to take part in organized outings to watch them return to land after a day of fishing. This type of tourism contributes to the increasing rarity of the species. Adults returning to their brood are disturbed by lights and camera flashbulbs.

bird have been counted.

The Whaler's route, which goes along the coast, is also a great place to see kangaroos and emus.

Australian sea lions and New Zealand fur seals are some of the species you can see here, and are a must-see for naturalists.

Observation

Whales in Australian waters are protected by a specific law. The Whale Protection Acts codifies relations between people and whales, and specifies the penalties incurred if these animals are disturbed.

Twenty-five species of cetaceans have been counted off the coast of South Australia, of which 17 live along the 124 miles (200 km)

87

The Aborigines

The Aborigines arrived in Australia at least 40,000 years ago. As hunters, fishermen, and gatherers, they acquired an amazing knowledge of nature that fed them for thousands of years. Even if their activity did modify their environment—the use of fire, for example, accelerated the disappearance of the giant wombat and the marsupial lion—this was nothing compared to 200 years of European colonization. During this period of time, more than 20 species of native mammals became extinct!

Animals play an important role in Aboriginal mythology, as they do in the legend of "Kondole, the whale": "At the time of the ceremonies, the day was so hot that drops of perspiration, rolling down the bodies of the participants, created all the rivers and streams in the area. The group did not know how to get the light it needed for its nighttime rituals. That is why it invited Kondole, the only possessor of fire, with the hope that he would bring it with him. But Kondole, in a bad mood, hid the fire in the forest before coming. Exasperated by his egotism, they all discussed the various ways in which to force Kondole to bring the fire to the ceremony. But he was a big, strong man and no one had the courage to face him.

"Finally, one of the participants lost control. He attacked Kondole by surprise and pierced his skull with his harpoon. Everyone was suddenly transformed into a different creature. Some became kangaroos, others opossums, and others even smaller animals. Some were transformed into birds, others slid into the water, becoming the fish that now populate the oceans. Kondole, the biggest of all, became a whale. That is why, since that time, it spits out a jet of water from the wound in its head." (Mounfort, *The Dawn of Time*, 1969.)

of coast that borders the vast Nullarbor Plain (some species are only known from strandings). The most common dolphins are the bottlenose, or large dolphin, and the common dolphin.

The first right whales arrive near the shore in May and the last leave the area in October. They spend the southern summer near Antarctica. In August and September, more than 100 right whales frolic in the area, with the total Australian population numbering 500 whales. These are primarily pregnant females, but also males and females ready to mate.

The cliffs and the dunes of Eyre's Peninsula offer magnificent promontories overlooking the whales along the coast, sometimes only 165 feet (50 m) from shore. The waters are so clear that you can see whales eating or playing. You can often see females accompanied by their young.

The best observation point, without a doubt, is the bay called Head of Bight, at the head of two small islands known as Twin Rocks, located 7 miles (12 km) from Route 1 (Eyre's route) in aboriginal territory. Each year, more than 30 calves are born there. These 19 miles (30 km) of coast are very important to right whales. There was a proposal in 1989 to classify this part of the coast as the Great Australian Bight Marine Park, but the proposed law has not been passed as of this date.

During this time of mating and birth, the whales become very demonstrative, and like to leap out of the water, while mothers play and frolic with their calves.

Still on Route 1 (Eyre's route), on the coast of Nullarbor National Park, other sites such as Wilson's Bluff and Merdayerrah Sand Patch are also worth a visit.

PRACTICAL INFORMATION

Distances in Australia are enormous—you will be surprised by how long its roads are.

88

TRANSPORTATION

■ **BY PLANE.** About a 22-hour flight from Los Angeles.

■ **BY CAR.** In Australia, it is easy to rent a car or to buy one for an extended stay and then sell it with several thousand additional miles on the odometer.

For families, it is also possible to rent campers, but they are expensive!

Road conditions are good in general, but secondary routes are lightly traveled and, in the event of a breakdown, you may have to wait a long time for help.

DISTANCES

Adelaide to Head of Bight: 682 miles (1,100 km)
Nullarbor to Yalata: 58 miles (94 km)
Port Lincoln to Yalata: 386 miles (622 km)

Route 1, which connects the best observation sights, crosses an area under the control of the Aborigines of the Yalata community.

You need authorization to enter it. You can get it at Nullarbor House if you are coming from the west or at

Yalata Road House if you are coming from the east.

The entry fee for the Twin Rocks observation site is $10 Australian, $5 for children. The money is used for the protection of this fragile site and for the maintenance of the road that leads to it.

The Yalata Whale Watch Center offers visitors a full range of services: crafts, fuel, camping, and groceries.

ACCOMMODATIONS

Ceduna, a stopover point for travelers in transit to Adelaide or en route to West Australia, has lots of campgrounds and hotels in all price ranges. Nullarbor House has a hotel and a place for campers.

Camping is possible in Nullarbor National Park, but a permit is required.

SITES

In Adelaide, a visit to the South Australian Museum is a must. This institution is responsible for whale research and for "controlling" the increasing number of tourists who have

come to whale-watch.

If you travel via Adelaide, make a detour to Victoria Harbour, 50 miles (80 km) south. A private organization, The South Australian Whale Center, offers sea excursions, a retrospective on the history of whaling, and an exhibit on the different species of whales.

A detour to the numerous caves painted by the Aborigines will complete the trip. The ideal is to rent the services of a local guide who can provide commentary on the engravings and paintings.

In western Australia, Monkey Mia is visited by some 40,000 people each year. They go to meet the Monkey Mia dolphins, a family of dolphins that swim very close to people. In the 1960s the dolphins started taking fish from people, and in 1986 rangers were stationed in the area to deal with the growing popularity of the site. Marine mammals are protected in most areas and any contact with individuals is restricted to official guidelines.

Observation Sites

Valdés Peninsula, Chubut, Argentina

The Valdés Peninsula is on Argentina's Atlantic coast. Situated in the province of Chubut, north of Patagonia, it is in fact an island connected to the continent by the Carlos Ameghino Isthmus, which is 22 miles (35 km) long. This strip of land is surrounded by two vast bays: Gulf San José in the north; Gulf Nuevo in the south. Gulf San José is classified as a reserve and boat access is regulated.

At the far end of Gulf Nuevo is one of Argentina's largest ports—Puerto Madryn. It is both an industrial center and a tourist location, with a population of 45,000 inhabitants. Located on the border of a deep water zone formerly known as Bahía Sin Fondo, it welcomes a large number of ships and is an obligatory stopover for tourists on the way to the Valdés Peninsula.

The interior of the peninsula is a remarkable geological phenomenon, constituting one of the largest depressions in the world, at 138 feet (42.1 m) below sea level. It is called Saline Grande. At its southern border, the little port of Puerto Pirámides, built in 1898 to export wool and salt, has preserved its native character, with white houses topped with red roofs. It is a major diving center and the departure point for whale-watching.

Flora and fauna

Bird Island, a provincial animal sanctuary that is not open to the public, is located half a mile (800 m) from the coast, in the Gulf of San José. With binoculars, however, you can see from the coast all the birds that mate there. Cormorants, Magellan oyster catchers, Dominican gulls, and steamer ducks have totally colonized the island's rounded formations.

Following the only road going north, you

89

Young elephant seals dueling in preparation for the more serious battles they will ultimately have when trying to create their own harem.

Killer whale attack on a colony of southern sea lions: the whales drift onto the pebbled shore to seize their prey, then leave when the next wave goes out.

The sand and gravel beaches at the foot of the large dunes are home to the only continental colony of elephant seals. Aggressive males arrive starting in July to select the best territories for themselves and to welcome a large number of females. These large seals are almost 20 feet (6 m) long and weigh 4 tons. They spend their time in violent and bloody combat. Upon their arrival, females give birth to a single baby that is completely black. The mother suckles it for a month before she abandons it.

Leaving Punta Norte, after 19 miles (31 km), Route 47 leads you to a large spit of land parallel to the continent. A lagoon has formed in this narrow depression. It is the Ansa Valdés, one of the richest areas in fauna, where Magellanic and flamingo penguins are found.

can see the white-crested guan. At the end of 62 miles (100 km) of this dusty road, you reach the southern tip of the peninsula, called Punta Norte, where killer whales and elephant seals live.

90

The Tehuelches

Before European colonists arrived, the province of Chubut and the Valdés Peninsula were populated by the Tehuelche Indians. They lived mainly by hunting armadillos, as well as collecting nandou and harvesting a number of species of plants. The coastal Tehuelches also ate crustaceans and mollusks.

They didn't have small boats to hunt the large whales that came close to the coast. They knew them, however, by those that were stranded and each time they took one to eat, it was an occasion for a great celebration.

In Tehuelche mythology, the whale was originally a land being, Goos:

"In olden days, a hero by the name of Elal who lived in Patagonia noticed that a large number of people were disappearing at a rapid rate. He assumed that Goos, the whale, was in some way involved. So he began to follow and observe. He found out that when the whale opened its mouth, it sucked in everything that surrounded it: horses, armadillos, foxes, men, and encampments.

"So Elal decided to intervene. He used his exceptional powers to transform himself into a horsefly, a large, annoying, and stubborn fly, got close to Goos, and allowed himself to be sucked in. Once inside the animal, he resumed his human form and discovered several survivors in the stomach. He reached for his knife to save them and cut a hole in Goos, letting everyone escape through this opening.

"So that the whale would no longer cause harm on land, Elal ordered him to leave for the bottom of the sea. That is why, since that time, whales live only in the sea."

Two and a half miles (4 km) off the road that connects with Puerto Pirámides, you can find a noisy colony of southern sea lions. These seals are large. Males weigh up to 770 lbs (350 kg) and are 6.5 feet (2 m) tall. They live at the foot of the cliffs. The males establish their territories on the hanging rocks and the gravel beaches. The females will arrive there to give birth in January and February. This site lets you admire the agility of these animals as they swim in the clear and turbulent waters of the Atlantic Ocean.

The road is bordered by many small shrubs that are the main source of food for livestock. The road comes out onto the little port of Puerto Pirámides, in which sea lions have made a home.

Observation

Whales start to arrive in May in the shallow waters of the bays, but the best time to see them is from July to October. They have just spent the summer scouring the Antarctic Ocean to build up food reserves and come here to mate.

By boat, they can only be seen in Gulf Nuevo.

They are very demonstrative. They hold their wide flippers, their tail, and their "bonnet" out of the water. Occasionally, they jump up and fall on their backs. They are friendly and come very close to small boats. In an inflatable dinghy or a kayak, you can touch them, but it is better to avoid contact.

Sailing cruises are certainly the most exciting way to whale-watch. Operators offer excursions of one to several hours. The prices are generally high and there are crowds—especially of Europeans.

Roger Payne, a cetologist who has spent several decades studying the right whale off the Valdés Peninsula, has developed a technique for identifying each individual by means of the position and size of the callosities on the top and the sides of a whale's head.

91

PRACTICAL INFORMATION

If you like small groups, avoid the larger companies and choose naturalist tourist agencies from the United States.

TRANSPORT

■ **BY PLANE.** From Buenos Aires, it is a two-hour flight to Trelew.

■ **BY CAR.** We don't recommended that you go to Patagonia with your own car on the only north-south route—Route 3. It is used by lots of trucks, and is the scene of many accidents. Gasoline is rare, with only one service station every 125 miles (200 km). Cars can be rented in Trelew and Puerto Madryn.

■ **BY BUS.** This is certainly the most economical way to reach the Valdés Peninsula. Buses leave Buenos Aires for the main cities in the area and regular service connects Puerto Madryn to the main tourist centers.

DISTANCES

Buenos Aires to Trelew: 880 miles (1,420 km)

Trelew to Rio Gallegos: 724 miles (1,167 km)
Trelew to Puerto Madryn: 38 miles (62 km)
Puerto Madryn to Puerto Pirámides: 60 miles (97 km)
Puerto Pirámides to Punta Delgada: 40 miles (63 km)
Punta Norte to Punta Delgada: 55 miles (89 km)

CLIMATE

The winds are violent and unpredictable.

ACCOMMODATIONS

There are several hotels in Puerto Madryn, one in Punta Delgado, and one in Puerto Pirámides where you can also possibly camp.

We recommend you watch the videocassette made by the staff of Oceanopolis, called *Ballenas*.

SITES

In Buenos Aires, the Argentine Bernardino Rivadavia Museum of Natural Sciences, located at 470, avenue Angel Gallardo.

From Rawson, after taking Route 3 and then Route 2 for 11 miles (18 km), the interpretation center and the Museum of the Carlos Ameghino Isthmus tell visitors about the flora and fauna they can see on the peninsula. As the center is located in the narrowest part of the isthmus, only 2.5 miles (4 km) wide at that point, you can see the sea on both sides. There is an observation tower from which you can view the sea.

The Punta Tombo Reserve, 74 miles (120 km) south of Trelew, has the largest colony of Magellanic penguins in the world—1 million.

Observation Sites

Cape Region, Cape province, South Africa

The region that is of interest for whale-watching is between Yzerfontein north of the Cape (33° 55' S latitude, 18° 22' E longitude) and Plettenberg Bay in the east, that is to say at the southwest tip of the Republic of South Africa.

This portion of the coast is situated at the confluence of two violent currents—the cold Benguela current, which comes from Antarctica and moves north, and the Algoa current, which travels south from north of Madagascar. The large difference in temperature between these two currents is responsible for significant differences in climate between the west and east coast.

The Benguela current, richer in nutrients, has led to an abundance of phytoplankton and, as a consequence of this, of other living

organisms (fish, birds, and marine mammals). The coast has few sheltering bays, with the exception of Saldanhubaai, Valsbaai, in the south of the Cape, and Table Bay, which was the location chosen for the first European settlement. Cape Alguhas (34° 50' S latitude, 20° 00' E longitude) marks the separation between the Atlantic and Indian Oceans. It is also the most southerly point of the African continent, which extends under water as the continental shelf.

Between the coast and the African plateau, a band 37 to 50 miles (60 to 80 km) has a Mediterranean climate, which has led to an abundance of vegetable and animal life.

Flora and fauna

There are many interesting species besides whales. However, South African reserves are really large parks that don't have access to the outside world. Even though they are extremely large, their scenery is wild, and their animals are "free," the space is still enclosed. Only birds and marine mammals can truly live the life of wild animals.

Penguins of the Cape were once abundant, but they have suffered from the massive exploitation of guano, the material they use to build their homes, and a tragic series of black tides. Their population has drastically declined.

There are lots of cormorants, of which there are three species dominated by the great cormorants of the reefs along the South African coast. Bird Island, opposite Lambert's Bay village, is home to an impressive colony of cormorants and Northern Gannets.

92

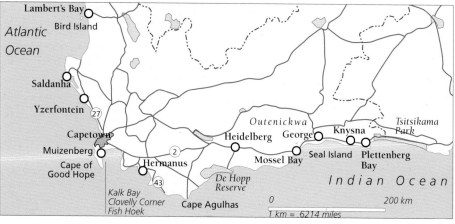

Kirstenbosch Botanical Garden.

Cape seals are very outgoing, and come together to mate and give birth.

Northern Gannets usually form mixed colonies with Cape penguins.

Although many capes and islands are called Seal Cape or Seal Island, no real seals live in this area. The name refers to fur seals. The Cape fur seal lives in about 20 colonies between Cape Cross in Namibia, in the west, and Algoa Bay, in the east. It was the first species on the southern African coasts to be heavily hunted, before hunters turned to whales. A small group of 2,000 seals found refuge on Seal Island, in front of Mossel Bay, which is also home to a colony of Northern Gannets and cormorants.

The De Hoope Reserve, located between the Cape and Mossel Bay, is devoted to nature appreciation. With seven different ecosystems alternating between lakes, waterfalls, and hills, this small territory is home to many sea birds, mountain zebras, and bonteboks, large South African antelopes. While there are many interesting animals on the coast, there are also animals inland that are worth seeing. Against the Outenickwa mountains, the forests of Cape Knysna and the Tsitsikama National Park contain astonishing floral riches. These sites are covered with large forests of indigenous species, such as yellowwoods, giant ironwoods, and stinkwoods, that are centuries old.

Numerous lichens, ferns, and mosses carpet these humid forests that are home to the Cape parrot, the semango monkey, the

93

The first navigators around Africa

Bartolomeu Dias was the first person to sail the entire length of the southern African coast.

Sent by the Portuguese king John II to find a sea route to the Indies, he sailed from Lisbon in 1487.

On December 1st, he passed Cape Cross, currently known for having the largest colony of Cape fur seals on Namibian soil. After seven days at sea, he came to what is currently known as Walvis Bay, the Bay of Whales, and, on February 3, 1498, after many navigational detours, entered Mossel Bay.

The accounts of the voyage summarily describe the fauna of the area: "This bay contains a small island that is populated by many large seals having shoulders, a neck, and a lion's mane. There are also numerous sea birds, larger than ducks, covered with feathers except on their wings, which prevents them from flying, with a cry resembling that of the

braying of an ass."

The navigators that followed in Dias's path encountered whales, as described in the report made by Jean Mocquet of his voyage to Mozambique and Goa, from 1607 to 1610: "On our arrival in Mozambique, we found out that our vice-admiral had passed the Cape of Good Hope after us, and that he had seen a marine monster pass alongside the ship, which had a strange shape and was of an enormous size; it breathed and snorted with much noise, and held its body in a circle, as a column, with a saddle on its back. As it passed close to the ship it made such a horrible noise that we thought we were done for, but finally it left us and we did not see it again." (Mocquet, *Editions Chandeigne*, 1996).

bush pig, and the blue duiker. More than 300 species of migratory birds have been counted. The Tsitsikama Forest National Park is known for its rare orchids, its Cape walnuts, and its wild banana trees.

Observation

The right whale has been protected in South Africa since 1940.

In 1988, new rules of conduct toward whales were established by the Sea Fishery Act. Approaching them by boat is limited to 980 feet (300 m) and if a whale appears closer than that, the boat must distance itself. In fact, some coastal sites are better for whale-watching traveling along Route 2 in Valsbaai, at Muizenberg Station, Kalk Bay (site of the first whaling station at the

beginning of the 18th century), Clovelly Corner, and Fish Hoek. You can also reach several sites if you leave the Cape and travel east (Route N2).

The De Hoope nature reserve at the end of Route 322, 25 miles (40 km) from Heidelberg, is rich in land animals, while its coast is often home to whales with their young.

Whale-watching is still relatively undeveloped here and the configuration of the coast prevents the establishment of many structures. Therefore, tourist activity has become concentrated at Hermanus. There are several providers there offering sea excursions.

North of the Cape, you can see whales in some locations, but you are less likely to. Bryde's whale, rarely seen at other sites, can be seen here. The area is also frequented by humpback whales, but only during February and March.

PRACTICAL INFORMATION

The best time to whale-watch is September.

TRANSPORTATION

■ BY PLANE. Several regular airlines fly from North America to Capetown. Once you are there, domestic airlines link George to the province capital.

■ BY CAR. In South Africa, driving is on the left, and distances are measured in miles. The road system is in perfect condition.

Route 2 leaves Capetown, and travels along the entire South African coast going east. There is no problem renting a car; all of the major companies offer cars ranging from small cars to campers, including 4 x 4 vehicles.

■ BY BUS. While many companies offer connections between towns, it is difficult to continue on to whale-watching points, which are often quite far away.

DISTANCES

Capetown to Port Elisabeth (Route 2): 557 miles (899 km)
Capetown to Cape of Good Hope: 37 miles (60 km)

Capetown to George: 273 miles (441 km)
Capetown to Hermanus: 62 miles (100 km)

ACCOMMODATIONS

You won't have any trouble finding accommodations in Capetown (bed and breakfasts, hotels, lodges, and motels). The whale-watching region is a popular vacation area for South Africans.

Many beach resorts there offer water sports and tourist attractions.

In Hermanus, there are several hotels but the easiest and best solution is the guest house.

CLIMATE

In winter (summer in Europe and North America) the weather in the Capetown area is humid and it often rains.

The coastal climate, east of Cape Agulhas, is different, with seasons less marked. Winter (May, June, July) is the driest period, with rain in the form of

brief showers occurring throughout the rest of the year. In September, at the elevation of the city of George, the temperature ranges from 46 to 64°F (8 to 18°C).

SITES

Southwest of Capetown, the Kirstenbosh Botanical Gardens are devoted to the preservation of indigenous species (almost 6,000).

In Mossel Bay, the Bartolomeu Dias Museum displays a replica of his ship and has an exhibit devoted to the first Portuguese, Dutch, and British navigators.

In Hermanus, the Old Harbor Museum is equipped with a telescope for observing whales. They can also be heard when they cross nearby.

Observation Sites

Bay of Fundy, New Brunswick, Canada

The Bay of Fundy is a large indentation that separates New Brunswick from Nova Scotia. It is shallow and has the biggest tides in the world, with an amplitude of more than 48.5 feet (14.8 m), the height of a four-story building. The water can rise 12 inches (30 cm) in 7 minutes! The rapid movement of these huge amounts of water has profoundly sculpted the landscape.

The origin of the bay dates back 350 million years, when tectonic movements caused a cave-in that was then covered by a warm, shallow sea. Forty-five million years later, the fault was filled in with sediment (sandstone and carboniferous marsh).

About 210 million years ago, new tectonic deformations caused volcanic eruptions. The earth's crust toppled over once again 195 million years after these violent changes, which altered the hydrological system. During the last ice age, about 10,000 years ago, glaciers planed down neighboring mountains.

Once the glaciers retreated, the sea once again poured into **95** the fault. This long history has left traces in the bay and a geological walk helps you imagine the intensity of these upheavals. On Grand Manan Island there are columns of basalt rising up from the sea, formed from the quick cooling of lava flows. They are reminders of a series of volcanic eruptions that were scattered along the Fundy rift. On the rocks of Hopewell

View of the Bay of Fundy at low tide in the area of Saint Martins, where many grottoes are carved into the cliffs.

Cape, the tide and ice sculpted the cliffs into arches, caverns, and monoliths.

The strong tides stir up the waters, helping the bay's teeming life. The violence of the currents form whirlpools, as in the Deer Island archipelago, "The Old Sow," the second biggest whirlpool in the world.

Flora and fauna

The Fundy National Park spans 80 square miles (206 km²) and contains an amazing diversity of environments: waterfalls, spruce forests, and cliffs overlooking the waters of the bay.

While the Bay of Fundy is an important whale-watching site, bird-watchers will love it too. More than 340 species of birds, 131 of which are nesting, have been counted on Grand Manan Island. Many migrating animals visit the bay where they find, in the islands, the silty estuaries, and the marshes, feeding sites, and meals to help them in their voyage between the polar regions and the southern United States or South America—Canada goose, kakawi duck, scoter, and thousands of sandpipers, including the semipalmated sandpiper and plovers.

Eiders and storm petrels rest in the small islands near Grand Manan. Machias Seal Island, a small island 12 miles (20 km) from Grand Manan, whose sole inhabitant is the lighthouse keeper, is home to 900 couples of monk puffins, guillemots, petrels, wheatears, and arctic terns. Access to the island is limited to a few visitors per year. Kent Island is populated by a colony of herring gulls and marine gulls.

The large amplitude of the tides has created a varied flora and fauna, able to adapt to the violent currents. Limpets, winkles, starfish, anemones, and sea urchins live on the rocks in the intertidal area.

Numerous algae, including the ascophylle with its floats in the form of grapes, are firmly attached to the rock. Each stage has its own flora and fauna, which lets you see very different bands of life. Look out for the incoming tide.

The climate conditions in the bay have favored the development of damp forests populated with large conifers and covered with various mosses and lichens.

Observation

In the Bay of Fundy, 17 species of whale have been counted, which, in addition to right whales, include fin whales, minke whales, and humpback whales, who are also

The Micmacs

The Micmac Indians were the most important group of people in the Maritime Provinces before the Europeans arrived. They assembled together in families to get through the winter and hunted deer, elk, bear, beaver, otter, seal, and, of course, walrus, which survived in this region until 1761. In the spring, they made maple sugar from the sap of maple trees. In summer, they fished for herring, sturgeon, cod, salmon, and eel. In summer, they wore loincloths with beads made out of bone or from whale baleen plates.

At the beginning of the 16th century, with the arrival of the Europeans, their way of life was considerably changed and many epidemics of smallpox decimated the population.

Nevertheless, the banks of the Bay of Fundy still resonate with Micmac legends and the god Glooscap. One of these legends tries to explain the origin of the formidable movement of the tides that characterize the bay.

According to legend, a whale, which was annoyed with the god Glooscap, struck hard with its tail, which made the waters of the bay move in a gigantic to and fro motion. The god Glooscap had to submit to the whale's power and from that time forth gave it control over the waters of the bay.

Here is another legend, "Why the whale chews its food": "Three canoes were crossing the bay when a whale caused them to overturn and ate the crews. Glooscap did not find this behavior acceptable. He put his hand on the whale's head and ordered him not to do it again. That is why, since that day, the whale is no longer capable of eating even a mackerel without having to chew it."

drawn in by the abundance of food. The expert observer will know how to recognize the shiny black back of the common porpoise or the pointed flipper of the Atlantic white-sided dolphin. Gray seals and harbor seals bask on the flat rocks.

Right whales can be seen in the bay from July to September. They come to take advantage of the abundant food supply, generated by the mixing of cold waters in the bay. Departing from Grand Manan or Deer Island, boat excursions are an easy way to see right whales. At East Quoddy Light, on the northern end of Campobello Island (near Deer Island), there is a good lookout for observing right whales. It is not easy to get to (you must take ferries), but between July and September the sightings are good. Several operators offer the usual motor boat trips, but you can also go on a day trip on an authentic schooner.

Recent data has shown that 100 whales mate and feed at the bay's entry point, near Brown Bank, off the coast of Nova Scotia.

Monk puffins are related to the great auk that once populated the region but are now gone. The monk puffin nests in a burrow carpeted with twigs.

97

PRACTICAL INFORMATION
Whales can be found in the bay from July to September.

TRANSPORTATION

■ **BY PLANE.** The closest airport from Montreal is that of Fredericton, capital of the province of New Brunswick. There are also connecting flights with Saint John.

■ **BY CAR.** It is easy to rent one. All sorts of cars are offered at prices that tend to be more expensive than in the United States.

There are good quality roads everywhere.

To reach Grand Manan, you must take the ferry at Blacks Harbour. The length of the trip, one hour and thirty minutes, gives you a chance to see whales. To reach Deer Island, you must take the ferryboat at Letete (one hour).

DISTANCES

Moncton to Saint John: 94 miles (152 km)

Caraquet to Saint John: 256 miles (413 km)
Montreal to Saint John: 582 miles (940 km)
Fredericton to Saint John: 64 miles (103 km)
New York to Saint John: 640 miles (1,032 km)
Boston to Saint John: 372 miles (600 km)

CLIMATE

The waters of the Bay of Fundy maintain a constant cold temperature.

Summer is cool. Winter is mild and humid. Fogs are frequent.

ACCOMMODATIONS

Campgrounds are generally well equipped. This is by far the most economical way, all the more so because tour operators offer combined camping/whale watching

packages. On Grand Manan, you can camp and hear the whales blow.

There are plenty of small hotels and family pensions in old houses along the whole length of Fundy's coastal route, from Saint Andrews, at the U.S. border, to Aulac, at the end of Nova Scotia, as well as on Grand Manan.

SITES

The Grand Manan Whale and Seabird Research Station, located on the northern tip of the island, has an exhibition center presenting the marine riches of the Bay of Fundy. A scientific team answers visitors' questions.

Do not forget to bring a mosquito repellent for your hikes inland.

Bowhead Whales
(Balaena mystecitus)

FRENCH: baleine franche boréale, baleine de Groenland
SPANISH: ballena franca

3 meters

The bowhead whale does not mind swimming under an icefield as long as it can break it in order to breathe. The white mark that appears at the base of the tail is only seen in some bowhead whales.

99

Description

Average length: 49 ft (15 m) with a maximum of 66 ft (20 m) for both sexes; newborn 11 to 14 ft (3.5 to 4.5 m). **Average weight**: 90 tons (maximum 110 tons); newborn weight unknown.

It is black. It has a white triangular mark on its chin, which is easy to see each time its head comes vertically out of the water or when the whale rolls over itself. Like other right whales, it does not have a dorsal fin. This is due to their adapting to swimming in ice-filled waters. Its flippers are short. A white area is sometimes visible on the tail.

Its jaw is particularly arched. The head is 40 percent of the body.

The blow forms a clearly visible 16-foot (4.9-m) V, characteristic of all right whales.

Behavior

Living in areas full of ice, the bowhead whale is well-adapted for lifting ice floes when it needs to breathe. It can break ice 7 inches (18 cm) thick, or even 24 inches (60 cm) according to some natives of the circumpolar regions, and can push the floes by using the top of its head near the blowhole. It can also detect and thus avoid areas of old ice that are too thick. In summer, it swims across open water with belugas and narwhals. During their migratory travels, some whales execute sequences of jumps during which all of their body, except for the tail, is projected out of the water, and then the whale falls back in on its side.

They sometimes hold their white chins out of the water.

Vocalizations

The sounds produced are located in the same range as that of the right whale—from 160 to 2500 Hz.

Traveling

The bowhead whale moves slowly, with a cruising speed of 6 mph (10 km/h).

Observations have shown that this whale sometimes uses the surface of its tail held widely, as a sail.

Migration

Bowhead whales don't travel very much, but instead stay on the fringes of the ice floes. They head northward during the summer and southward when the ice floes approach.

Diving

Depth reached: more than 650 feet (200 m); length of time between 10 and 20 minutes.

Feeding

This whale's diet consists exclusively of small crustaceans that it filters through its particularly long (8.5 ft [2.6 m]) and numerous (an average of 225 per jaw) baleen plates. When feeding it can consume between 1 and 2.5 tons of food per day.

One of the ways right whales feed is by coming together in a group of six or seven and swimming in a V formation. They move on the surface at a constant speed, mouths mostly open to hold the animalcules on their baleen plates.

Longevity

The lifespan of bowhead whales is 40 years.

Reproduction

Mating takes place in spring. Gestation lasts 10 to 12 months. Births take place in midwinter, when the whales seek refuge in the south.

Distribution

Bowhead whales stay in the highest latitudes in the Northern Hemisphere. Scientists think they can identify four distinct populations, which are distributed between the Bering Strait and Franz-Josef Land, passing by the Sea of Beaufort, the north Canadian archipelago, the coasts of Greenland, of Svalbard, and all the way to the New Siberian Islands. Another group may visit the northern part of the Sea of Okhotsk.

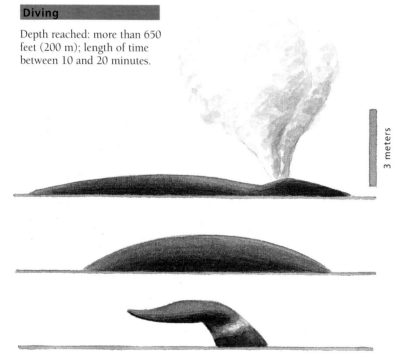

3 meters

Population

After being hunted for many years, its world population today is estimated at 8,000 whales. Protected since 1931, bowhead whales have become more abundant, and all recent data is optimistic, especially concerning the group in the Davis Strait.

History

Quite plentiful in polar waters prior to the arrival of the Europeans in the 15th century, the bowhead whale was already rare in the 17th century after having been widely hunted.

In 1607, Henry Hudson noted in his trip reports that in Spitzberg the whales frolicked like carp in a fishpond. This observation tolled the knell for the northeast Atlantic population and began a veritable stampede toward Spitzberg. Hundreds of boats carrying thousands of men arrived to hunt the whales. Each summer, in the archipelago's northwest, a small town was set up: Smeerenburg, the "city of fat."

At the beginning of the 18th century, there were no longer any bowhead whales there. It was to hunt bowhead whales that Frobisher, Davis, and other navigators of the 16th and 17th centuries ventured through the maze of the north Canadian archipelago. Bowhead whales in the Bering and Okhotsk Seas were fortunately left alone.

101

Emerging close to a small boat, with its stomach in the air, this bowhead whale is showing the white mark on its chin, which is characteristic of the species.

Observation sites

Clyde River area, Baffin Island, Canada

The Clyde River is located on the west bank of Patricia Bay, in the Clyde Inlet, on the east coast of Baffin Island (70° N latitude, 68° W longitude).

The Baffin Island platform is made up of ancient rock, like the rest of northern Canada.

This land is a polar region today; however, in the past, this land was submerged under shallow waters that deposited large layers of sediment. The land resurfaced into a temperate climate, and was covered with lush vegetation. Sixty million years ago, tectonic upheavals separated Greenland from the mainland, evidence of which can still be seen on the Baffin Island coast.

The successive ice ages that followed rubbed away the volcanic and sedimentary substrata leaving only the ancient rock.

Freed 8,000 years ago from the glacial mass that covered it, the earth's crust moved up. This is why there are ancient beaches at altitudes of 656 feet (200 m). Only two icecaps remain on Baffin Island: the Barnes icecap and the Penny icecap.

The Clyde River is the only area from which you can see bowhead whales and the only one that is set up for tourists. The small village is home to 600 residents of Inuit origin. Its Inuit name is Qangittugaapik, which means Pretty Cove. It is surrounded by hills and bordered by a pebble beach. The main employment is hunting, specifically seals and caribou, but many hunters are magnificent whalebone sculptors.

This region was visited by whalers until the end of the 19th century. Commercial hunting stopped at that time because the whale number had decreased so much that there were no more bowhead whales in the area.

102

Flora and fauna

Polar bears are common in this region; therefore, visitors have to be extremely careful when traveling on foot and setting up camp.

While there are a lot of caribou inland, they are, however, difficult to see. Since they are constantly being hunted, caribou are timid and quickly flee.

The polar fox and the lemming are the only species of land mammals that are easy to see.

During sea excursions, you can see marble seals, one of the bear's favorite foods, and the Inuit's main game, and ringed or hooded seals.

An arctic tern hovering over the water as it looks for food.

103

It is only toward the end of August that the icefield is briefly dislodged from the bottom of the Baffin Island bays.

Emerging bowhead whale.

Thule Culture

The current occupants of Baffin Island are the descendants of a group related to Thule culture that spread from the west to the east across the Canadian Arctic between the years 950 and 1300. These people, who lived in houses built of whale bones, lived a life based on bowhead whale hunting in Alaska and on the shores of the Beaufort Sea.

In the 10th century, a significant warming of the climate caused the edge of the summer icefield to move northward. Until then, the Arctic was populated by the Dorset people, isolated in northern Canada for 3,000 years. The disappearance of ice allowed whales to come in close and feed near the shore. The Thule people followed them.

The Thule started to move further out from where they were. In order to hunt bowhead whales, the Thule traveled as far as northern Greenland, across the maze formed by Banks, Victoria, Melville, Cornwallis, and Devon Islands. The second wave of expansion took place around Baffin Island and northwest of Hudson Bay.

The Thule hunted whales in small fleets, consisting of umiaks (large skin-covered canoes able to carry a dozen people) and kayaks and using powerful harpoons that enabled them to fix skin floaters on the back of the animal. When Martin Frobisher and John Davis explored Baffin Island at the end of the 16th century, Thulean culture was still thriving.

An abrupt change in climate at the beginning of the 19th century, known as the "small ice age," put an end to their way of life, based on hunting bowhead whales. Massive bowhead hunting by Europeans and Americans was the end of the Thule.

Ancient sled runners made of whalebone (north coast of Baffin, J.-M. Dumont collection).

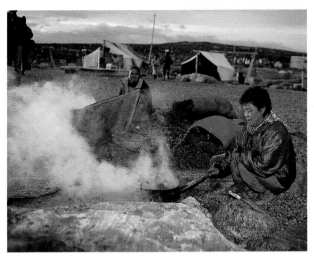

Each summer, the Clyde River Inuit leave their village to return to their traditional hunting and fishing grounds.

Observation

In August, when the icefield becomes dislodged, about 60 whales feed near the shores of Baffin Island.
    Cape Christian is one of the best places to watch them blowing.
    Narwhals, in migratory herds of over 100 whales, travel along the northern coast of Baffin Island. This can take up to two days, from the first whale to the last. You will need a local guide if you want to go whale-watching. Use an American tour operator as an intermediary, who can guarantee the quality of the local service.

Lots of birds come to take advantage of the riches of the arctic summer. Arctic terns nest in the gravel and welcome the overcurious visitor with sharp cries and pecks with its beak. The arctic char is abundant in the rivers and easy to fish. The vegetation is that of the northern tundra. It is made up of mosses, lichens, and flowering plants that have adapted to the rigors of the climate. Arctic poppy, eight-petal dryas, and dwarf willow result in a short, but colorful flowering period (end of July, beginning of August).

Known for being placid, right whales are above all masses of muscles, so you must be careful. Do not get in the way of their path. In 1995, an inflatable dinghy was overturned by a whale, resulting in the death of three tourists.
    The WWF works with the Clyde River community to track the bowhead whale population and to protect them during their seasonal stay in Isabella Bay.

105

PRACTICAL INFORMATION

There is only one way to get to Baffin Island: by plane.

TRANSPORTATION

■ **BY PLANE.** Regular flights go as far as Iqaluit. From there, small planes fly regularly to Clyde River.

DISTANCES

Montreal to Iqaluit: 1,270 miles (2,054 km)
Iqaluit to Clyde River: 465 miles (750 km)
Clyde River to Broughton Island: 217 miles (350 km)

ACCOMMODATIONS

When you are camping, be very careful in areas where there are polar bears.
    The Quammaq Hotel has room for 12 people. It also has a restaurant.

CLIMATE

The average temperature is 44°F (4°C) in July and −12°F (−26°C) in January.
    The dominant winds are northwesterly.
    The icefield lasts from October to August.
    Precipitation is light but, in these latitudes, it can snow during the summer.

SITES

Not all of the archaeological sites have been identified in the Northwest Territories; therefore, be very careful if you find an ancient object. Leave it there.
    Tourism is focused on char fishing and on different types of crafts: silk scarves, table linens, and sculptures.

Sperm Whales
(Physeter macrocephalus)
FRENCH: cachalot, macrocéphale,
physétère, grand souffleur
SPANISH/PORTUGUESE: cachalote

Description

Average length: male 49 ft (15 m) (maximum 66 ft [20 m]); female 36 ft (11 m) (maximum 56 ft [17 m]); newborn 13 ft (4 m).
Average weight: fully mature males weigh 40 tons (maximum 45 tons); females weigh 22 tons; newborns weigh 1 ton.

The sperm whale has a single blowhole, located on the front left end of the head. The head is large and in an adult represents one-third of the total body length.

When viewed from above, sperm whales look flat; however, when viewed from the side, you can see that they are perfectly rectangular.

The lower jaw is narrow, in the shape of a very elongated Y and, located at the very base of the head, appears relatively small. Sperm whales have between 36 and 58 teeth that don't have enamel and are conical in shape. Teeth first appear at about age ten. Some teeth occasionally start to grow on the upper jaw but rarely break through the gum. The flippers are short. There is no dorsal fin but, two-thirds of the way down the body, there is a series of four to seven flat bumps of decreasing size. The tail is long and triangular in shape, with a ridge in the middle.

Sperm whales are gray black, and some have white around the mouth. White marks on the stomach of older whales seem to grow larger with age, which may mean that an old white male like Moby Dick could exist.

Behavior

Sperm whales have highly intricate social relations. In areas close to the tropics, females and their young stay in groups while males migrate to higher latitudes. Young bachelor males form

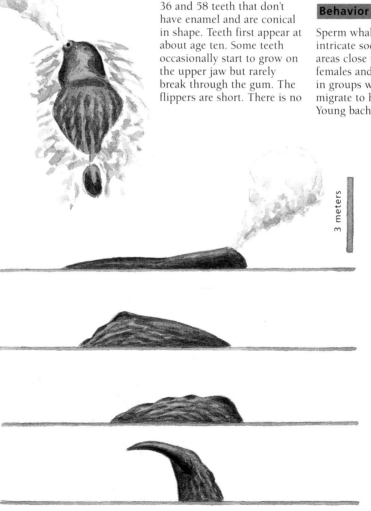

3 meters

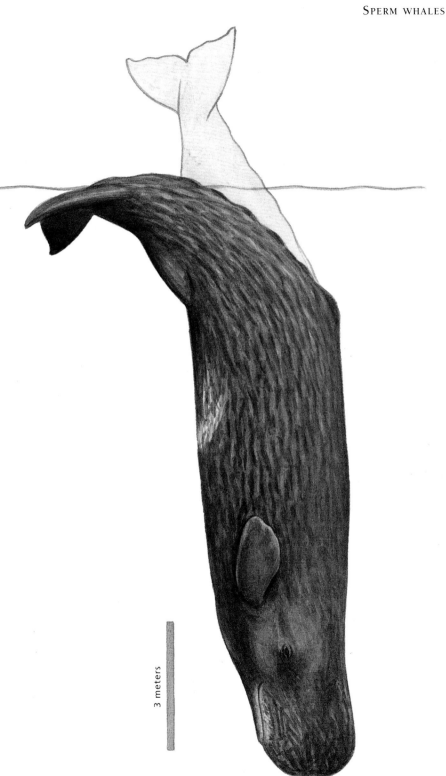

3 meters

small groups that travel together, while those that are physically and socially mature travel alone. During mating season, males challenge each other and sometimes fight in order to create a harem over which they jealously keep guard. When they are resting on the surface, groups of female sperm whales and their young occasionally allow themselves to be observed at a very close distance, as long as you approach them calmly and use oars.

Traveling

The sperm whale travels at about 6.2 mph (10 km/h), but can reach speeds of 28 mph (45 km/h) when fleeing.

Vocalization

Recorded for the first time in 1957, the sounds produced by the sperm whale are between 200 and 32,000 Hz and consist of rumbling, creaking, and sharp "clicks." Scientists are nearly certain that some of these sounds are used for echolocation, especially in the dark depths where the animal hunts. The fact that observers have seen a blind individual whose stomach was full corroborates this thesis.

Diving

The sperm whale can dive to depths greater than 7,380 feet (2,250 m) and stay underwater for 90 minutes. It dives straight down, at a speed of 4 to 5 mph (7 to 8

km/h) and resurfaces at about 6 mph (9 km/h) at nearly the same place. This seems to mean that sperm whales lie in wait for their prey.

Migration

The two sexes move away from the equator in spring. While the females stay in areas that are close to the tropics, males migrate in summer to higher latitudes.

Feeding

Sperm whales mainly eat squid, especially giant squid, but will go for smaller squid if they don't have a choice. Sperm whales may finish off their meals with some tuna, barracuda,

The sperm whale's amazing head

An adult male's head is enormous and can be up to one-third of its total length. And while all toothed whales have cranial dissymmetry, due to nasal bones that have moved left, the sperm whale has pushed this dissymmetry further than all of them.

The blowhole—all toothed whales have only one—is located on the front left end of the head, which gives its blow a unique shape that comes out toward the left. The path of the nasal passages, once you get past the bony portion, is amazing. This is explained by the fact that a sperm whale's enormous head case is not only used for focusing sound waves, but is also used as ballast.

The case contains a very specific type of oil, spermaceti. This oil was once much sought after by whalers. It turns to liquid at 92°F (33°C), when the sperm whale is on the water's surface. To dive, the sperm whale cools this oil down by reducing the circulation of blood in this part of the skull, and making water circulate in the case. This is done using the right nasal passage that opens

up into two vestibular sacs in the front and the back of the case, which open up under the base of the case into a passage that is not very wide, but is about 3 feet (1 m) long.

This quickly brings the spermaceti to its congealing point, at about 90°F (31°C). While slowly congealing, the spermaceti becomes more dense and helps anchor the sperm whale, which allows the sperm whale to easily stay at a certain depth because it has zero buoyancy. This explains why it can dive vertically at a speed of about 4 to 5 mph (7 to 8 km/h) and then reappear practically in the same place when it returns to the surface at 6 mph (9 km/h).

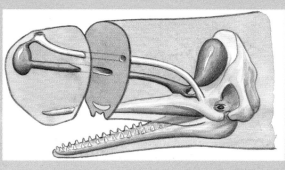

or shark, in order to reach its daily ration of 1 to 1.5 tons.

Longevity

Since toothed whales have teeth that continue to grow throughout their lives, you can guess their age based on the number of layers of teeth, just as you can calculate the age of a tree by counting the number of circles in its trunk. The oldest sperm whale on record was 70 years old but the average age for sperm whales is about 35 years.

Mating

The sperm whale is sexually mature at about 10 years old,

The giant squid

The giant squid has long been a legendary monster. People imagined a titanic battle in the blackness of the abyss until the giant squid was eaten by the sperm whale. The giant squid (*Architeutis princeps*), however, really does exist. It is 66 feet (20 m) tall and has 10 tentacles, of which two, longer than the others, are used as arms. An adult can weigh 1 ton. It lives so deeply in the sea that fishnets can't reach it. All we know about it comes from incomplete or partially decomposed specimens found in the stomach of sperm whales, presumably its only predator. Using underwater robots, scientists think that the *Architeutis* may be fairly common in dark, deep sea.

but males must reach their full maturity, about 25 years old, to be able to establish a harem. Real battles take place over possession of these harems, which often consist of more than 20 whales. Gestation lasts 16 months. Lactation lasts from 1 to 2 years.

Distribution

The sperm whale is an animal of the open sea, and can be found in all the oceans of the world, from the equator to the tip of the ice fields, but only males frequent the higher latitude areas. Females rarely go beyond 40 degrees from the equator.

Population

The world population is currently estimated to be at least 450,000.

111

History

The value of whale products made them highly sought after, and as technology improved more boats went in search of them. American whalers mainly hunted sperm whales up until America stopped hunting whales in 1925. Spain and Portugal stopped hunting whales in 1984, when they joined the European Community and an international moratorium on whale hunting was set up.

Possible confusion

When it dives, the sperm whale's tail leaves the water, like that of a humpback whale, but the sperm whale's tail does not have white markings.

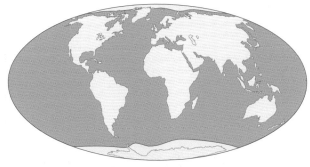

The triangular tail with its central ridge and the blow swerving to the left are the two main characteristics of the sperm whale.

Observation sites

Pico Island, Azores Archipelago, Portugal

The Azores archipelago is made up of nine volcanic islands with a total area of 900 square miles (2,335 km). The archipelago rose up from the ocean floor on the Atlantic ridge at the same latitude as Lisbon and at more than 930 miles (1,500 km) from the European mainland.

This archipelago of timeless island-gardens extends over 370 miles (600 km) from east to west and probably appeared fairly recently, only 15,000 years ago.

Situated in the central group, Pico Island owes its name to the peak that

overlooks it—a currently dormant volcano—and that, at 7,700 feet (2,350 m), is the highest point in Portugal.

The archipelago was uninhabited until it was discovered at the beginning of the 15th century and its colonization began in 1439, shortly thereafter in Pico (1460). Pico is the second largest island (172 square miles [447 km²]) in the Azores but has only 16,000 inhabitants while the total population of the archipelago is 237,000.

Whaler's bay.

Corvo

Flores

Graciosa

Atlantic Ocean

Terceira

Faial

Madalena

Cais do Pico

São Jorge

Pico

Azores archipelago

São Miguel

Misterio da Santa Luzia

São Roque do Pico

2531 m

P i c o   I s l a n d

Misterio do São João

Misterio da Silveira

São João   Silveira

Lajes do Pico

Vigia da Queimada

Santa Maria

0   10 km

1 km = .6214 miles

0   100 km

Flora and fauna

The local flora and fauna is made up for the most part of introduced species, but some small shrubs, which grow in altitudes above 1,970 feet (600 m), are endemic, like the Canaries laurel, the viburnum, and the Azores holly.

Volcanic Pico has a strange landscape made up of vast, desolate lava fields, the *misterios*, evidence of the most recent eruptions.

Observation

Since 1984, the Azores have been a peaceful haven for the sperm whale herds that pass the summer there each year. The Azores are surrounded by very deep plains and are

The imposing silhouette of a volcano overlooking Pico Island.

113

The Azorian whalers

First hired by American whalers who came to the Azores to find cheap crew members, the Azorians, starting in 1830, hunted sperm whales themselves. The sperm whales came to the deep waters—almost 2.5 miles (4,000 m) deep— surrounding the archipelago. This hunting became a cottage industry that lasted up until the 1880s. Except for the use of small motor boats to tow the carcasses, the methods they used remained practically unchanged for one and a half centuries. Once a sperm whale was seen from land, it was chased in a sloop from which it was harpooned by hand. The wounded animal would tow its pursuers until it was exhausted, then the hunters would kill it with a spear before bringing it to the factory. Today, because of Portugal's entry into the European Community, sperm whales are no longer threatened in this area. If the occasional former whaler goes out to sea, it is only to whale-watch.

Azorians sculpted miniature reproductions of whaling instruments out of whalebone (J.-M. Dumont collection).

located at the border of the warm and cold waters of the North Atlantic. The Azores are far away from any major merchant marine routes, and are not frequently visited by vacationers.

It is mainly females, often accompanied by their young, who were born in the Azores, that can be seen, from May to September. Sea excursions depart from Lajes, according to whale sightings made on land, which generally happen around ten o'clock in the morning, as they did in the era of whaling. Some days, when the whales are particularly receptive, you can even slip into the water with them.

In the archipelago's waters there are 15 other species of whales, among which are the common dolphin, the bottlenose dolphin, the Atlantic spotted dolphin, and the tropical pilot whale.

It is also possible to find the fin whale and, more rarely, the Sowerby's beaked whale or bottlenose whale.

PRACTICAL INFORMATION

The best time to see sperm whales is from May to September.

TRANSPORTATION

■ **BY PLANE.** Only flights by TAP, Portugal's national airline, can land in the archipelago, a two-hour flight from Lisbon. They land at Ponta Delgada, on São Miguel Island. From there, you can take a plane or a boat to Madalena, the principal city on Pico.

Today, Lajes do Pico, on the island's southern coast, is the whaling capital of the archipelago. You can get to it by taxi or rental car.

DISTANCES

The island is 26 miles (42 km) long and 9 miles (16 km) wide. Places are very close together!

CLIMATE

The weather is unpredictable and there is a local saying that you can experience four seasons in a single day. This is caused by cold currents coming from the north and mixing with the Gulf Stream. Because of the Gulf Stream, the water temperature is always between 64 and 70°F (18 and 21°C) (unfortunately, the coast is not suitable for ocean bathing), while the air temperature varies during the year from 55 and 77° F (13 and 25°C). Fortunately for whale-watchers, the best time to see sperm

whales is from May to September, which is also the driest season of the year. Just the same, you should bring rain gear as well as lightweight clothing, along with a sweater for evenings or for climbing in Pico.

ACCOMMODATIONS

Madalena and Lajes do Pico have several hotels and small pensions of basic comfort, but the staff is always friendly. Simply ask, and you will be answered with a smile.

There is a campground in Lajes, behind the church.

SITES

Pico Island still has seven watchtowers as well as several unused whaling plants from its whaling days. You can visit one in Cais do Pico, on the northern coast, now converted into a whaling industry museum. The small port of São Roque do Pico, also on the northern coast, is also worth a visit.

On the opposite coast, Lajes do Pico has a very interesting Whaling Museum, which is also the departure point for a trip that lets you get close to sperm whales.

After the museum, a 3-mile

(7-km) walk (taking three hours) shows you both la Vigia da Queimada—the closest watchtower to Lajes, which dates from 1939 and was restored for whale-watching—and the Fabrica de Baleia, the town's former whaling plant. The trail is marked with yellow markers.

Also, do not miss a walk in the misterios, those mysterious lava fields only seen in Pico (misterios of São João and da Silveira on the southern coast, and of Santa Luzia on the northern coast).

Since you will pass by there anyway, stop for several days on São Miguel Island, the largest in the archipelago. It has several beautiful crater lakes. The best known is that of Sete Ciudade, 19 miles (30 km) northwest of Ponta Delgada. The islands of Fogo, the same distance east, and especially that of Vale de Furnas, a bit further in the same direction, are equally remarkable. The capital, Ponta Delgada, with its pretty little squares, is known for its exotic gardens.

114

Kaikoura, South Island, New Zealand

New Zealand is made up of two large islands, and is located on the Pacific fire belt, 1,240 miles (2,000 km) from the Australian coast. While the North Island is volcanic, South Island, with a more pronounced relief, is made of sedimentary rock—sandstone and schist—that has been folded by moving tectonic plates, and deeply chiseled by the most recent ice age. Both islands have mild and humid weather, favorable for the development of densely foliated forests. These forests are home to unique flora and fauna as they consist of species that are found nowhere else, not even in Australia.

Flora and fauna

The New Zealand fur seal, a marine animal from the pinniped order, takes advantage throughout the year of the vast deserted beaches surrounding Kaikoura to bask in the sun. As its name indicates, it is also an endemic species.

Before man's most recent arrival in New Zealand—around the year 800—there was only one land mammal: a bat. People brought rats, dogs, cats, and livestock, which, all together, considerably changed the biotope and caused the extinction of a number of native species. One of the most remarkable was the moa, a giant bird 13 feet (4 m) tall, which was heavily hunted in the Kaikoura area.

One of the last existing representatives of the numerous species of apters that once populated these islands is the shy kiwi. It is a well-known symbol of New Zealand, but can rarely be seen outside of zoos.

The eastern coast of South Island is also a good location place, for those who are patient, to see birds that adapted to the sea in very much the same way as whales did. They are three relatively

115

Whales help the Maoris

Maoris arrived in the Kaikoura around 850 A.D. They immediately believed that whales were the reincarnation of deceased humans. To the Maoris, whales were their sea companions that helped them while they fished or during bad weather.

Their attitude toward whales took a turn for the worse with the arrival of European colonists. In the 19th century, the relations between the Maoris, unemployed for the most part, and other New Zealanders was particularly tense at the beginning of the 1880s. In 1987, the Kati Kuri clan of the Ngai Tahu tribe succeeded in raising funds to create a company simply called "Whale-Watch TM," which has exclusive rights to sperm whale-watching. The number of visitors in Kaikoura has increased from 3,400 the first year of operation to 188,000 in 1995. The company is the main employer in the area and the Maoris of Kaikoura have thus regained pride from the new-found respect for their traditions.

The reef heron fishes on the seashore.

Fur seals rest on the flat rocky areas. Once hunted for their fur and their fat, they are now completely left alone and are now common in the Kaikoura region.

unknown species of penguins—those birds that lost the ability to fly the same way that whales lost the ability to live on land. The crested penguin and the yellow-eyed penguin are quiet and not very friendly. They are not easy to see in the large covering of vegetation where they live. The third is the little blue penguin, which is only 18 inches (45 cm) tall and is the smallest member of the penguin family. It is mainly active at night.

And of course, there are many other birds, one of the most remarkable of which is the royal albatross.

The primary forests, which are still intact and grow on South Island, are mainly made up of evergreen southern beeches and conifers, with a dense undergrowth of lianas, epiphyte plants, and treelike ferns. In some dry areas of the coastal zone, there are large grassy tufts of tussoc, a plant often found on subantarctic islands.

For those even a little interested in botany, New Zealand is a universe that is both rather rich and totally new. A change of scenery to be sure!

Observation

New Zealand waters are full of whales. The small village of Kaikoura, located almost at the geographic center of the country, on South Island, is particularly known today as a paradise for observing sperm whales, which can be approached at sea all year round. Situated at the foot of the Southern Alps, Kaikoura is frequented by whales because the seabed, near the coast, is deeper, descending more than 1 mile (1,600 m) down.

A number of other whales frequent this part of the Pacific: humpback whales, fin whales, killer whales, pilot whales, common dolphins, bottlenose dolphins, and Risso's dolphins, to name only a few. Two remarkable species habitually stay in the area around Kaikoura: the dusky dolphin, native to southern waters, and the Hector's dolphin, a species that exists only in New Zealand waters.

117

PRACTICAL INFORMATION

Sperm whales can be seen in the Kaikoura area all year round.

TRANSPORTATION

New Zealand is far; you can only reach it by plane. Maybe you can stop there on a tour of the world. Most flights to New Zealand land in Auckland, on North Island. Some international flights also fly to Wellington and Christchurch. Estimate a maximum of 26 hours of flying time. Once there, it is easy to travel to any part of the country by plane, boat, bus, or rental car. Kaikoura, a small village of 3,000 inhabitants, is located on South Island, practically in the geographic center of the country, 124 miles (200 km) north of Christchurch. It can be reached from Wellington by plane, a 25-minute flight, or by train, a 3-hour trip. Coming from Christchurch, estimate 5 hours by bus or by train.

DISTANCES

Christchurch to Kaikoura: 118 miles (190 km)
Auckland to Kaikoura: 370 miles (600 km)

CLIMATE

Remember that summer in the Southern Hemisphere corresponds to winter in Europe. New Zealand, a country of islands, does not experience extreme temperatures. The differences in temperature between winter and summer is usually no more than ten degrees. In the area of Kaikoura, the average temperature in January is between 68 and 77°F (20 to 25°C). In July, it is between 50 and 60°F (10 and 15°C). And the sun shines 2,000 hours per year.

SITES

There are far too many things to see in New Zealand to be able to list them all here. New Zealand has 13 national parks and 3 marine parks.

If you are going via Christchurch, do not miss the Botanical Gardens, reputed to be the most beautiful in the country, and the International Antarctic Center, next to the airport.

As for the Canterbury Museum—right next to the Botanical Gardens—you can learn all about Maori culture and the now-extinct giant moa.

APPENDICES

Identification at sea

• If you see a large whale with a straight blow, a curved dorsal fin that you can see when the blowholes disappear under water:
- If the whale's dorsal fin seems very small, its back is not arched when it dives, but its tail appears above the surface, you are looking at a blue whale.
- If, when the whale dives, the rear of the whale's back is arched and you can't see its tail, you are looking at a fin whale.

• If you see a large whale, straight blow, shapeless dorsal fin, highly arched back as it dives, tail raised, white marks on its underside, you are looking at a humpback whale.

• If you see a large whale, bent blow on the very front of the body, dorsal fin made up of a succession of bumps that decrease in size,

120

Waving its flipper, this humpback whale seems to be signaling to the tourists who have come to admire him.

large tail visible at sounding, you are looking at a sperm whale.

• If you see a large whale, vertical blow that spreads out, dorsal fin made up of a succession of bumps that decrease in size, a small tail that is visible at sounding, you are looking at a gray whale.

• If you see a large whale with a double blow that is V-shaped, and no dorsal fin:
- If the whale is entirely black, with callosities on its head, you are looking at a right whale.
- If the whale has white marks at the front of its head, you are looking at a bowhead whale.

• If you see a medium-sized whale, blow barely visible, curved dorsal fin visible at the same time as the blowholes, tail invisible, you are looking at a minke whale.

Appropriate conduct

Whale-watching is like trying to uncover a secret, in this case, the secret of the largest mammals on our planet. But you must have the greatest humility and respect when approaching whales. Here are some simple rules that you should follow.

Never follow whales using motor boats. Instead, wait for them to welcome you. Never impose your presence. Unless accompanied by specialists and if the approach is made using oars, stay at a distance of at least 330 feet (100 m), particularly with females accompanied by their calves. Getting between a mother and her calf can result in an accident, particularly with gray whales. Never cut off a whale at less than 980 feet (300 m). Divers should not get into the water less than 98 feet (30 m) away from whales. Even if they are inoffensive, whales are enormous compared to humans, and you have to give them time to integrate a "little runt" into their universe.

Whale-watching in a plane should be done at an altitude of at least 980 feet (300 m), and whale-watching in a helicopter, even at this altitude, is not advised. The sound and the waves created by the whirling of the blades are significant stress factors.

Do not go into birthing areas, such as the lagoons of Baja California, the San José Gulf, the Valdés Peninsula in Argentina, and the Lahaina Channel (Hawaii).

For a sea voyage, seek out competent individuals with demonstrated experience. At most of the sites, scientists organize trips that provide you with both security and information that are indispensable for a truly fascinating voyage. Look for whale-watching companies with on-board naturalists or cetacean scientists. Often these specialists can provide valuable information and entertainment between whale sightings. And be sure to pay attention to the many interesting birds along the shore and out to sea. An ornithologist could be invaluable. While you may be tempted to make the trip with a native (Baja California) since it is often less expensive and seems more interesting, their boats are not always of the highest quality.

Sea kayaks are a wonderful sea craft to whale-watch in, as long as you follow all the safety rules for this type of craft, and take appropriate precautions when you approach large whales.

Before you venture into bays where there are whales, find out about local laws, authorizations that may be necessary, and specific precautions you must follow regarding tides, currents, and storm risks.

Do not forget that, at many sites, you see whales from the coast. In South Australia especially, but also in California, you must remain perfectly calm. Whales often come very close to the beach and may be disturbed by noise. Too many tourists contribute to the acceleration of the erosion of dunes and coastal vegetation. Tourists should follow paths, should not pick plants, and should not leave behind film containers or used batteries.

Underwater encounter with a right whale. Underwater contact can only be done by scientists.

Protecting whales

The large whales have been hunted since the 10th century. Over time, hunting and dismembering techniques have evolved into industrial methods and the number of whales has continued to decline since the 17th century.

Hunters began chasing the species that were easiest to kill, such as the right whale and then the gray whale. Sperm whales have been hunted since the 18th century. Rorquals, which are faster, were not bothered until the beginning of the 20th century, with the advent of the harpoon gun with an explosive head, the inflating of cadavers to keep them on the water's surface, and factory boats capable of hoisting the large whales on board for dismembering.

Starting in 1946, it was decided to limit the take by instituting a system of quotas. Unfortunately, these quotas were fixed in "blue whale units," in which one blue whale is equal to two fin whales or two and a half humpback whales, which has resulted only in limiting the mass hoisting on board whalers of all species mixed together. Humpback whales have been protected since 1966, but it was not until 1967 that the blue whale was protected, at a time when the population had reached such a minimum level that some believed would lead to its extinction. Analysis of DNA from whale meat sold in Japan has recently shown that blue whale meat was being fraudulently sold as minke whale, a small rorqual, the only species for which hunting is still authorized.

In the mid-1970s, the hunting quotas were drastically reduced, heralding protective measures that would be followed in the 1980s.

In 1982, a moratorium was adopted by a vote of 25 to 7 of the member countries of the Whaling Commission, but it was not put into effect until 1986. Iceland stopped whaling in 1986. Only Japan and Norway continue to hunt the minke whale under cover of obscure scientific research.

121

In 1994, whaling was prohibited in Antarctic waters.

Today, the Whaling Commission is still subject to pressure from the countries in favor of whaling, such as Japan, Iceland, and Norway.

A string of small islands support these large countries in order to be able to trade with them, islands such as Antigua, Saint Lucia, Grenada, Solomon, and Dominica. Each country has been able to draft specific laws or decrees for regulating the relations between whales and people, specifying the approach distances and the behavior of observers when whales are present.

Exceptions have thus been made for native populations that traditionally hunt

Off the Bahamas, scientists practice a crossbow biopsy on a humpback whale.

whales as a source of food in Siberia, Alaska, and Canada. These exceptions were unfortunately distorted in Siberia, where whales were hunted to provide food for animals being raised for fur.

While the actions of the International Whaling Commission were exemplary for the large whales, they forgot about the small ones. Dolphins and pilot whales are still being hunted more and more, as in the Faro Islands, for example.

Preparing for your trip

In the United States
Visit the whale exhibit at the Museum of Natural History in New York. Mystic, Connecticut, offers a host of historical and scientific information to whale-watchers.

In France
In the Great Hall of the Museum of Natural History in Paris, there is a sperm whale skeleton positioned at the beginning of its dive into the water. The right whale skeleton provides a good illustration of the residual pelvis, while models of small whales help you estimate the size of different species. The main library of the museum is open to the public and contains many ancient and modern works on the history of whales and whale biology.

In Normandy, at Luc-sur-Mer, a humpback whale skeleton is exhibited in the town park.

The Oceanopolis center in Brest, dedicated to the sea, is particularly interesting for its teaching approach. Numerous projections and exhibit panels provide information about marine life and specifically about marine mammals.

The Museum of the Sea in Biarritz (on the Esplanade des Anciens-Combattants) provides visitors with numerous whale models and skeletons, as well as a diorama depicting whale hunting.

In Belgium
The Royal Museum of Natural History in Brussels has a very complete and well-presented collection of skeletons of all the large whales (as well as a number of the smaller whales).

In the United Kingdom
In the city of Hull, the Town Docks Museum has the most complete collection in Europe of objects related to whaling.

Whale-watching

Equipment

A good pair of binoculars is indispensable. On a boat, it is better to have binoculars with low magnification (the first number on your binoculars), either 7-times or 8-times magnification. It is fairly tiring to look through binoculars for long periods of time on a small boat that is moving and may result in seasickness. If you are planning to use your binoculars at sea a lot, make sure they are watertight against sea spray and streaming water. Only binoculars that focus without external movement are waterproof.

On land, a telescope is very useful. Often used for bird-watching, it is only effective if mounted on a stable base (at sea the wind can cause the telescope to vibrate). A good sun visor is also very useful. Magnification should not be too large—a 20-times or 25-times eyepiece is good. Also, bring a guide for identifying birds in the area and perhaps a guide to visible marine mammals. These are often small booklets put together by associations or scientific bodies, and are usually very well done and inexpensive, which makes them indispensable for an observation trip. A raincoat and rain pants, a pair of boots, and even a hat and a pair of gloves should be part of a whale-watcher's equipment.

If your tour operators are serious, they will provide you with life jackets on small boats and a floating suit in very cold waters (such as the Saint Lawrence). For larger boats, life jackets must be accessible and the crew is required to show you where they are located. If you suffer from seasickness, bring medicine for it, because it can hamper your watching and ruin a good trip.

Photographing whales

Taking good pictures of whales is not easy. In most cases you will be disappointed. The photos tend to be blurry because of movement or incorrect focus. You'll have pictures without whales because you took the photo too early or too late. A whale appears only briefly, and it usually shows only its back, sometimes a tail, more rarely a full body during a breaching out of the water. In addition, few boats offer the opportunity to hang over the water safely. All are constantly moving. As a general rule, use a 24 x 36 camera equipped with a small 7- to 12-inch (18- to 30-cm) telephoto lens with a grip or a chest harness.

A polarizing filter is useful as it cuts

A rare sight among right whales—an albino calf with its mother, off the Australian coast.

down on reflection but it "eats" a lot of light, which means you should use 100 or 200 ASA film.

A UV filter is indispensable at sea and also protects the lens from sea spray. Note that automatic focus cameras can be disturbed by the blow and the reflections. All equipment must be protected in a waterproof bag or, at least, in a solid plastic (garbage) bag. At the end of the trip, the camera and the lenses must be cleaned to remove oily traces left by the ocean air and sea spray.

On land you have to have a very long telephoto lens, at least 16 inches (41 cm) on top of a stable base.

123

Vocabulary

English	French	Spanish	Portuguese
back	dos	lomo	dorso
baleen	fanon	barba de ballena	barba de baleia
binocular	jumelles	prismáticos	binòculos
blow	souffle	soplo	sopro
blowholes	évents	arificio nasal	eventos
blubber	graisse, lard	grasa	gordura
breaching	saut	salto fuero del agua	salto para fora de àgua
calf	baleineau	ballenato	bezzero
callosity	calosité	callosidad	calosidado
case	melon	caja, melón	melào
deep	profond	profundo	profundo
dolphin	dauphin	delfín	golfinho
elephant seal	éléphant de mer	elefante marino	elefante marinho
fin	aileron	aleta	barbalana
flipper	nageoire	aleta	nadadeira
fluke	lobe caudal	lobulo caudal	lobo caudal
fur seal	otarie à fourrure	foca peluda	otària
gray amber	ambre gris	ambar gris	ambar cinzento
gull	goéland	gaviota	gaivota
harpoon	harpon	arpón	arpào
head	tête	cabeza	cabeça
herring	hareng	arenque	arenque
killer whale	orque	orca	orca
mating	accouplement	acoplamiento	acasalamento
mussel	moule	mejillòn	mexilhào
pilot whale	globicéphale	calderón	boca-de-palena
porpoise	marsouin	marsopa	boto
pregnant	gravide	preñada	gràvida
rostrum	rostre	rostro	rostro
rubber boat	bateau pneumatique	barca de caucho	barca pneumatico
scar	cicatrice	cicatriz	cicatriz
seal	phoque	foca	foca
sea lion	lion de mer	león marino	leào do mar
shark	requin	tiburón	tubarào
shallow	peu profond	poco profundo	pouco profundo
shrimp	crevette	camarón	camarão
sloop	chaloupe	chaloupa	chalupa
sounding	plongée	sondeo	mergulho em profundidade
sperm whale	spermaceti	esperma de ballena	espermacete
spy-hopping	observation de surface	observación de superficie	observaçào de superficie
squid	calmar	calamar	lula
stranding	échouage	varar	encalhar
suckling	allaitement	cria	aleitemonto
tail	nageoire caudale	aleta caudal	nadadeira caudal
teeth	dents	dientes	dentes
whaler	baleinier	balenero	baleeiro
whaling	chasse à la baleine	caza de balenas	caça à baleia
whale-watching	observation des baleines	observación de ballenas	observaçào das baleias

Glossary

Baleen: horny plates in a baleen whale's mouth, used to filter small food organisms from the water.
Benthic: related to the bottom of the sea, or to that which lives on the bottom of the sea.
Blow: visible projection of liquid particles in the atmosphere when a whale breathes on the surface.
Blowhole: external opening of nasal passage.
Cetologist: specialist in whales.
DDT: dichloro-diphenyl-trichloroethane, pesticide that biodegrades with difficulty, becoming concentrated at each successive level of the food chain.
Diatom: one-celled alga with calcareous or silicic skeleton.
DNA: deoxyribonucleic acid, chemical basis of heredity and basic component of chromosome chains.
Echolocation: orienting or navigating by means of reflected sounds.
Heterodont: possessing different teeth.
Hyperphalangia: multiplication of the number of phalanges.
Katabatic wind: localized movement of air, caused by the rapid chilling of a mass of air upon contact with a glacier and the abrupt descent of this air to a lower zone.
Krill: large zooplankton, consisting of different species of crustaceans; in the Antarctic region, krill consists primarily of Euphausia superba, at 1/4 inch (6 cm) long it is one of the largest species of euphanisiids, able to reach a density of more than 77 lb (35 kg) per cubic meter of water.
Melon: frontal organ of toothed whales, consisting of an oily mass acting as a lens for focusing sounds emitted by the animal.
Microplankton: extremely small plankton.
Monocular: term that describes the vision of an animal when the fields of vision of the two eyes do not superimpose on each other.
Myoglobin: muscular protein similar to hemoglobin, which, like hemoglobin, has the ability to attach to oxygen.
Oligodont: having few teeth.
PCB: polychlorinated biphenyl, a group of organochloric products used by various industries; concentrated by phytoplankton, they enter into the food chain where they follow a process of bioaccumulation.
Pelagic: of, pertaining to, or living in, open oceans.
Peribular: that which surrounds the tympanic bubble of the auditory system.
Petroglyph: drawing carved into stone.
Phylogeny: genealogical tree of an order, a suborder, a species.
Pluriradicular: term that describes a tooth with several roots.
Polyodont: possessing numerous teeth.
Rostrum: in whales, the upper part of the head, between the tip of the muzzle and the melon in toothed whales.
Sounding: "Diving," when this action is made by a whale leaving the surface for the depths.
Teuthophageous: squid-eating.
Uniradicular: term that describes a tooth with a single root.
Upwelling: an upwelling zone occurs when a current causes cold water that is rich in nutrients to rise to the surface.
Zooplankton: animal plankton (as distinguished from phytoplankton, plant).

125

Bibliography

Books
O. Abel, *Les Odontocétes de Boldérien (Miocène supérieur) des environs d'Anvers,* musée royal d'Histoire naturelle de Belgique, 1905.
Aristotle, *Histoire des animaux* (Livres I à X), Les Belles Lettres, 1964-1968.
P. C. Beaubrun, *Atlas préliminaire de distribution des cétacés de Méditerranée,* Musée océanographique de Monaco, 1995.
J.-Y. Cousteau and Y. Paccalet, *La Planète des baleines,* Robert Laffont, 1986.
J.-Y. Cousteau and Y. Paccalet, *La Mer de Cortez,* Flammarion, "L'Odyssée" collection, 1988.
A. G. Credland, *Whales and Whaling: The Arctic Fishery,* Shire Publications, 1982.
T. Du Pasquier, *Les Baleiniers français de*

Louis XVI à Napoléon, Henri Veyrier, 1990.

M. Foucart, Terres Australes. Péninsule Antarctique et Terre de Feu, GNGL, Travel Book, 1995.

J. Geraci & D. Saint-Aubin, Sea Mammals and Oil: Confronting the Risks, Academic Press, 1990.

H. & R. Gerson, The Bowhead Whale, Fisheries and Oceans/WWF Canada, 1986.

E. Hoyt, The Worldwide Value and Extent of Whale Watching 1995, Whale and Dolphin Conservation Society, 1995.

M. Judd, C. Kemper, J. K. Ling & J. Olman, A Guide to Whales and Whale Watching in South Australia, South Australian Museum, 1993.

S. K. Katona, A Field Guide to the Whales, Porpoises and Seals of the Gulf of Maine and Eastern Canada, Charles Scribner's Sons, 1983.

R. Kellog, A Review of the Archeoceti, Carnegie Inst., 1936.

S. Krauss & K. Mallory, The Search for the Right Whale, Crown Publishers Inc., 1993.

L. Lacroix, Les Derniers Baleiniers français, Editions maritimes et d'outre-mer, 1968.

R. Marion & J.-P. Sylvestre, Guide des otaries, phoques et siréniens, Delachaux et Niestlé, 1993.

B. H. & E. McConnaughey, Pacific Coast, The Audubon Society Nature Guides, 1986.

H. Melville, Moby Dick, Gallimard, 1980.

S. Moss, Natural History of the Antarctic Peninsula, Columbia University Press, 1988.

Oceanic Society, Field Guide to the Grey Whale, Sasquatch Books, 1989.

Pliny the Elder, Histoire naturelle, Livre IX, Les Belles Lettres, Paris, 1955.

C. Scammon, The Marine Mammals of the Northwestern Coast of North America, based on the 1874 edition of John Carmany and Company, Dover, 1968.

I. Shapiro, The Story of Yankee Whaling, Harper & Row, 1959.

G. Soury, Dauphins en liberté, Nathan, 1996.

P.-J. Van Beneden, Recherches sur les squalodons, Académie royale de Belgique, 1865.

L. Watson, Whales of the World, Hutchinson, 1981.

L. K. Winn & E. Howard, Wings in the Sea, The Humpback Whale, University Press of New England, 1985.

Periodicals

M. R. Clarke, "The Head of the Sperm Whale," Scientific American, Vol. 240, no. 1, January 1979.

F. C. Fraser & P. E. Purves, "Hearing in Cetaceans," in: Bull. British Mus. (Nat. Hist.) Zoology, Vol. 7, no. 1, 1960.

P. D. Ginderich, B. H. Smith, & E. L. Simons, "Hind Limbs of Eocene Basilosaurus: Evidence of Feet in Whales," Science, 1990.

J. Kanwisher & S. Ridgway, "L'Echophysiologie des cétacés," Pour la Science, August 1983.

H. Nelson & K. Johnson, "Les Laboureurs du fond des mers," Pour la Science, no. 114, pp. 50–57, April 1987.

R. Payne, "Humpbacks: Their Mysterious Songs," National Geographic, January 1979.

R. Payne, "New Light on the Singing Whale," National Geographic, April 1982.

R. R. Reeves & E. Mitchell, "Current Status of the Grey Whales, Eschrichtius robustus," Canadian Field Naturalist, vol. 102 (2), pp. 369–390, 1988.

J. Tuck and R. Grenier, "Une station baleinière basque du XVIe siècle au Labrador," Pour la Science, January 1982.

T.J. Walker, "The California Grey Whale Comeback," National Geographic Magazine, vol. 139, no. 3, pp. 394–415, 1971.

H. Whitehead, "Les Sauts des baleines," Pour la Science, May 1985.

B. Wursig, "Les Baleines: des mammifères très sociaux," Pour la Science, no. 128, pp. 90–97, 1988.

Videocassette

Ballenas, "Raconte moi la mer" collection, Océanopolis, 1995.

CD-ROMs

Whales and Dolphins, Ramson, 1996.

Les Océans, Microsoft, 1995.

En compagnie des baleines, Découvertes Multimédia, 1993.

Le monde sous-marin, Edusoft, 1995.

Sound Recordings

Songs and Sounds of the Humpback Whale, 1987 (recordings made in Hawaii and in Baja California).

127

Acknowledgments
We would like to warmly thank the
following people who helped us put together
the documentation we needed:
Argentina: Marina Mittelman and Marie
  Foucard
Australia: South Australian Whale Centre
Azores (Portugal): Serge Vialelle
Belgium: Jacques Dumont, Johan Gezels, as
  well as the staff of the Institut royal des
  sciences naturelles de Belgique
Canada: Diane Rioux
Egypt: Dr. Mohamed A. El-Bedawi, Director
  of the Egyptian Geological
Museum of Cairo; Catherine and Baudouin
  Dupret
Japan: Hiroshi Furuya
New Zealand: Monica, of Dolphin Encounter
  (Kaikoura)
Norway: Olav Akselsen
Spain: Asumpta Gual, Juan Carlos, Jimenez-
  Marin, Miquel Pontes

Work completed with the help of
Anne Cauquetoux
Stéphanie Houlvigue

Picture research
Rémy MARION

Picture credits
J.-L. ALBOUY (GNGL): p. 101
S. BONNEAU: p. 55
G. DIF: p. 59
J.-M. DUMONT: pp. 10, 17, 23, 28 top, 28
  bottom, 60, 69 bottom, 104 bottom
E. CHAUCHE (STOCK IMAGE): p. 72 top
A. COMPOST (BIOS): p. 26
M. COSSEC: pp. 103 bottom, 104 top, 105
J.-P. FERRERO (PHO.N.E.): pp. 74, 121
F. GOHIER (PHO.N.E.): pp. 6, 8–9, 16, 18,
  20, 21, 24–25, 30–31, 35, 37, 44–45, 49,
  58, 62–63, 67, 69 top, 80–81, 90 top,
  106–107, 111, 118–119
O. GRUNEWALD: pp. 27, 38 top, 70, 76 top,
  85, 86, 87 top, 87 bottom, 115, 116 top,
  116 bottom, 120, 122
H. and JEANSSON: p. 41 bottom
C. and L. MARION: pp. 22, 41 top, 53,
  54 top, 54 bottom, 76 bottom, 77, 78 top,
  78 bottom, 79, 89, 90 bottom, 93 bottom,
  95, 97, 103 top, 113 bottom
MUSÉE DE L'HOMME COLLECTION: p. 42
  (cl. M. Delaplanche): p. 72 bottom
OCEANOPOLIS: p. 29
R. SMYTH (PHO.N.E.): p. 123
G. SOURY: p. 113 top
K. STIMPSON (STOCK IMAGE): p. 71
K. TOURNIER (STOCK IMAGE): p. 93 top
J. J. WOOD (STOCK IMAGE): p. 112
A. ZIEBELL (PHO.N.E.): p. 48